# The Measure of a MAN

## Gene A. Getz

## Regal Books

A Division of GL Publications
Ventura, California, U.S.A.

## Other good reading by Gene A. Getz:

*When You're Confused and Uncertain* (Abraham)
*When Rejection Persists* (Joseph)
*When Your Goals Seem Out of Reach* (Nehemiah)
*When Your Job Seems Too Big* (Joshua)
*When You Feel Like A Failure* (David)
*When the Pressure's On* (Elijah)
*When You Feel Like You Haven't Got It* (Moses)

Published by Regal Books
A Division of GL Publications
Ventura, California 93006
Printed in U.S.A.

Library of Congress Catalog Card No. 74-175983
ISBN 0-8307-0291-1

**19 20 21 22 23 24 / 91 90 89 88 87**

Rights for publishing this book in other languages are contracted by Gospel Literature International (GLINT) foundation. GLINT also provides technical help for the adaptation, translation, and publishing of Bible study resources and books in scores of languages worldwide. For further information, contact GLINT, Post Office Box 488, Rosemead, California, 91770, U.S.A., or the publisher.

# Contents

## WHY THIS STUDY?

Though the New Testament letters say more about the functioning church as a *corporate* entity than it does about *individual* Christians, the fact remains that a mature church is made up of individuals—Christians who are each developing the mind of Christ—particularly at the leadership level. Paul outlines clearly in 1 Timothy 3 and Titus 1 a profile by which *each* of us can measure our personal level of maturity.

## RENEWAL—A BIBLICAL PERSPECTIVE

Renewal is the essence of dynamic Christianity and the basis on which Christians, both in a corporate or "body" sense and as individual believers, can determine the will of God. Paul made this clear when he wrote to the Roman Christians—"be transformed by the *renewing of your mind*. Then" he continued "you will be able to test and prove what God's will is" (Rom. 12:2). Here Paul is talking about renewal in a corporate sense. In other words, Paul is asking these Christians as a *body* of believers, to develop the mind of Christ through corporate renewal.

Personal renewal will not happen as God intended it unless it happens in the context of corporate renewal. On the other hand, corporate renewal will not happen as God intended without personal renewal. Both are necessary.

The larger circle represents "church renewal." This is the most comprehensive concept in the New Testament.

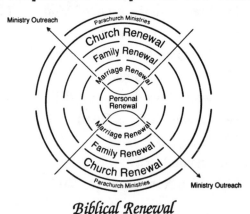

*Biblical Renewal*

However, every local church is made up of smaller self-contained, but interrelated units. The *family* in Scripture emerges as the "church in miniature." In turn, the family is made up of an even smaller social unit—*marriage*. The third inner circle represents *personal* renewal, which is inseparably linked to all of the other basic units. Marriage is made up of two separate individuals who become one. The family is made up of parents and children who are also to reflect the mind of Christ. And the church is made up of not only individual Christians, but couples and families.

Though all of these social units are interrelated, biblical renewal can begin within any specific social unit. But wherever it begins—in the church, families, marriages or individuals—the process immediately touches all the other social units. And one thing is certain! All that God says is consistent and harmonious. He does not have one set of principles for the church and another for individual Christians. For example, the principles God outlines for local church elders, fathers and husbands regarding their role as leaders are interrelated and consistent. If they are not, we can be sure that we have not interpreted God's plan accurately.

The books listed below are part of the Biblical Renewal Series by Gene Getz designed to provide supportive help in moving toward renewal. They all fit into one of the circles described above and will provoke thought, provide interaction and tangible steps toward growth.

| ONE ANOTHER SERIES | PERSONALITY SERIES | THE MEASURE OF SERIES |
|---|---|---|
| *Building Up One Another* | *Abraham* | *Church* |
| | *David* | *Family* |
| *Encouraging One Another* | *Joseph* | *Man* |
| | *Joshua* | *Marriage* |
| | *Moses* | *Woman* |
| *Loving One Another* | *Nehemiah* | |

*BIBLE BOOK SERIES*
*Ephesians, Philippians, 1 Thessalonians, Titus, James*

*Sharpening the Focus of the Church* presents an overall perspective for Church Renewal. All of these books are available from your bookstore.

# A WITNESS!

It is not often that I have had an opportunity to be involved in a "happening." Usually an event of this nature is a unique and very brief experience. But I was involved in a twenty-week happening!!

Over the years, I have attended many challenging and helpful in-depth Bible studies. But no study so convicted me of my shortcomings or gave me such a solid basis for concrete changes as this study of leadership qualifications in 1 Timothy 3 and Titus 1.

As an elder in another church I had reviewed these qualities from time to time and even discussed them in depth with other Christian men. Since there is nothing mystical about the terms, and the meaning of each qualification seems to be clearly stated, I felt I had a very good "handle" on the biblical standards for an elder.

Only through a comprehensive study of each of these qualities, however, did I begin to understand their full impact and their broader application as the standards for *any* mature man of God. Moreover, an interesting personal phenomenon has occurred. While being convicted of shortcomings and focusing on needed changes in my own life, I have had more peace than at other times in my life. Since this last year has not been without at least its share of pressures, problems, and other disquieting factors, I feel that God has granted an inner peace which has hopefully been accompanied by changes observable by business associates and personal friends.

Changes generated through biblical application must start on the inside and work themselves to the exterior. Sometimes, therefore, others only received glimpses of this change. I have, however, seen marked changes in many of the others who have participated with me in this "happening." Properly applied, I know this study can have a powerful impact on your life and I covet this experience for you.

Donald Kerr

Donald Kerr, chairman of the board, the Kerr Companies, Real Estate Development and Brokerage, lives in Dallas, Texas. He helped start several Fellowship churches in the Dallas area and has also been active in serving on the boards of Dallas Theological Seminary, Trinity Christian Academy, Christian Family Life and Pine Cove Christian Conference Center. He is also a member of the board of directors of the Center for Church Renewal, an organization directed by Gene A. Getz.

WHY THIS?

This book emerged out of a dramatic experience in Bible study and sharing with a group of laymen in Dallas, Texas. A number of these men now serve with me as elders at Fellowship Bible Church—also in Dallas.

On twenty successive Thursday mornings, from 6:45 to 7:45, we met in a conference room at the Downtowner Motel, before all of us went off to work for the day. Our goal was to discover from Scripture and from each other how we could become more mature men of God.

The twenty characteristics and qualities of maturity specified by the apostle Paul in 1 Timothy 3:1-7 and Titus 1:5-9 formed the basis for our study. Each week one of us took about 30 minutes to share what the Scripture had to say about a particular quality, which was followed by approximately 30 minutes of discussion and personal sharing, with a particular focus on *how* each one of us could better develop this quality in our lives.

The personal experiences and struggles of various men in the group had a profound impact on all of our lives. As I helped lead these sessions, as I listened and participated as a member of the group, my own heart was stirred to share some of these truths with other men. Hence, this book! Its inspiration grew out of a life-changing experience.

Although the written presentations which follow vary considerably from the material used by the men who led these discussions, I want to express appreciation to each of the following men who initially opened the Scriptures and led each discussion: John Breneman, Joe Hill, Lee Jagers, Don Kerr, Don McWhinney, John Maisel, Bruce Miller, Bob Norwood, Doug Powell, Ken Thomson, Jim Walta, and Jim Westgate. I would also like to thank Dr. Phil Williams, Professor of New Testament Literature and Exegesis at Dallas Theological Seminary, who read this manuscript and offered many helpful suggestions.

Each of these men and many others in the group ministered in a special way to my own life and to each other. Our vocations differed. Our life goals varied. But we had one thing in common—our personal struggles, as well as our victories in Christ. As we studied the Scriptures and shared our lives with each other, both of these experiences became a dynamic source of mutual encouragement and challenge to become more and more like Jesus Christ in all areas of our lives.

For all of us this is just a beginning! Won't you join us in our journey toward maturity in Christ? Paul expressed it well: "Not that I have already obtained it, or have already become perfect, but I press on in order that I may lay hold of that for which also I was laid hold of by Christ Jesus" (Phil. 3:12).

GENE A. GETZ

# HOW TO USE THIS BOOK

Each chapter in this book is self-contained, presenting a biblical mark or characteristic of Christian maturity. At the end of each chapter there is a personal project designed especially to help you develop this particular quality and make it part of your lifestyle.

You can study each chapter *on your own* and work out each project as you go. Better yet, read it *with your wife* or close friend and work out the projects together. Or you can combine this approach with a *group study*. Share the leadership responsibility in the group. Take one chapter for each discussion meeting. Use the book as a springboard into the Scriptures and then discuss your findings. Culminate with a sharing session on *how* to become the kind of person described in each chapter. Then have each member of the group follow through at a personal level by working through each project.

A final word! Remember the words of Paul as you read and study: "All Scripture is inspired by God and profitable for teaching, for reproof, for correction, for training in righteousness; that the man of God may be adequate, equipped for every good work" (2 Tim. 3:16,17).

# WHERE WE'RE HEADED

We're living in a day of instant formulas that supposedly can be applied to everything under the sun from TV dinners to "how to get rich" in three easy lessons. Our "push-button society" and computerized age have conditioned us to think of "presto-chango" solutions to a multitude of problems.

When it comes to spiritual maturity, some Christians have also fallen prey to this instantaneous-type thinking. Be "filled with the Spirit," say some and that is the secret to the victorious Christian life! "You must abandon and crucify all self," say others, and then you'll suddenly rise to a new level of spirituality. Or, more recently, we're told to "discover our spiritual gifts" and begin to function in the body of Christ as God intended. Along with these ideas, of course, go the Bible reading and prayer formulas.

Now all of these statements are worthy of careful consideration. But in themselves they are vague generalizations that frequently confuse new and older Christians alike. As I reflect back on my own life as a Christian, I can remember trying most of these formulas, but usually with a certain degree of disappointment in the results.

I have come to realize there is no quick shortcut to "becoming a man of God"—the thesis of this study. All of us, of course, embark on our Christian journey with a variety of backgrounds and experiences —which affect the progress we make in our Christian life. But one thing is sure, no matter what our spiritual and psychological heritage, it *takes time and effort to become a man of God.*

## HOW TO RECOGNIZE A MAN OF GOD

But what is a man of God? How do we recognize a spiritually mature person?

These are not new questions. This was a problem in New Testament days. When Timothy stayed in Ephesus to help the Christians mature, he came face to face with men who wanted to be teachers and spiritual leaders in the church. Paul commended those who wanted to lead. "It is a fine work he desires to do," wrote the apostle (1 Tim. 3:1). "But," he implied, "make sure he is a *certain* kind of man."

Titus, too, faced this problem. Paul specifically left him in Crete to "appoint elders in every city" (Titus 1:5). And again Paul implied, "But make sure each man is a *certain* kind of man."

The two passages in Paul's letters to Timothy and

Titus form a powerful profile for testing a Christian's maturity level (1 Tim. 3:1-7; Titus 1:5-10). The following is a combined list of these spiritual qualifications:

1. Above reproach
2. Husband of one wife
3. Temperate
4. Prudent
5. Respectable
6. Hospitable
7. Able to teach
8. Not given to wine
9. Not self-willed
10. Not quick-tempered
11. Not pugnacious
12. Uncontentious
13. Gentle
14. Free from the love of money
15. One who manages his own household well
16. A good reputation with those outside the church
17. Love what is good
18. Just
19. Devout
20. Not a new convert

Paul got beyond generalizations to those specific characteristics that are marks of a man of God. Here is a person who has become a man of God through a process of spiritual growth and development over a period of time. He has learned to reflect Jesus Christ in his total life-style.

It is certainly implied that this man "has put off the old man" and "put on the new." He has abandoned those attitudes and behavioral patterns that were connected with his former pagan life-style, and has adopted those attitudes and behavioral patterns that are Christ-like. *But* it is also obvious that this has been the result of a process of becoming more and more conformed to the image of Jesus Christ.

Note, too, that in this entire list there is no reference to spiritual gifts.[1]

Paul did not say look for men with the gift of pastor-teacher, or the gift of administration, or the gift of helps, or the gift of exhortation. In fact, there is very little reference to an ability or a skill. Rather, out of the twenty qualifications listed, nineteen have to do with a man's reputation, ethics, morality, temperament, habits, and spiritual and psychological maturity. And the other one has to do with his ability to lead his own family.

There is an unfortunate bewilderment among evangelicals regarding spiritual gifts. I've seen some of the men I work with struggle with this problem. Some have been given the idea that they must discover their spiritual gifts before they can begin serving Jesus Christ. Unfortunately, this is putting the cart before the horse. The Bible teaches that we must begin by *becoming a man of God.* We must begin where Paul began. If one desires to be a spiritual leader in the church, it's "a fine work" he desires to do. But we must make sure we have developed the qualities that are specified in 1 Timothy 3 and Titus 1.

I have often challenged my students at Dallas Theological Seminary to set forth as goals in their own lives the qualifications for leadership specified by the apostle Paul. It is relatively easy to evaluate a person's fitness for the ministry on the basis of academic criteria. Can he exegete the text? Can he prepare a good sermon? Can he preach and teach well?

All of these, of course, are excellent goals, but not basic qualifications. I would much rather work with a man who is qualified spiritually and psychologically than one who has lots of skill and is yet carnal. A man who has the qualities set forth by the apostle Paul can quickly develop skills and use them for the glory of God. However, the man who has lots of skill but is yet carnal has the potential to lead people in the wrong direction.

This is not to downgrade education. We need all the training we can get. But in all of our training if we do not develop basic qualifications for spiritual leadership, we are certainly unprepared to be a servant of Jesus Christ.

This fact, incidentally, has significant implications for churches looking for a minister. Judgments are often made on how well he can preach or teach, and not on what he *is* as a man, which has frequently led to tragic consequences.

## WHY THESE CRITERIA?

I have chosen these characteristics from 1 Timothy and Titus for several reasons.

First, they appear to be normative for spiritual leaders today. They are spoken regarding men who are to function at the local church level in a permanent capacity.

The second reason for selecting these characteristics is that they appear to be qualities that every Christian—particularly every Christian man—should strive for. Paul states in both his letter to Timothy and his letter to Titus that if "any man" desires to be an elder, it is a fine work he desires to do. But make sure, says Paul, that he is a certain kind of man measuring up to certain standards. In other words, these qualities seem to be goals for *every* Christian man. Some men will possess these qualities and serve as an elder or bishop.[2] Other men will possess these qualities, but will not necessarily feel called or have the time to serve in this spiritual capacity. The qualities, however, are goals for every Christian man.

A third reason for choosing these characteristics is that these qualities enumerated by Paul form a composite profile that is complete and comprehensive. Obviously, this was his intent when he prescribed this list. Here truly are the marks of a man of God! Paul brings together in these passages many characteristics of spiritual maturity that are scattered throughout the New Testament. In fact, as will be shown in this study, the majority of these twenty traits are prescribed elsewhere in the Bible for *every* Christian, including women.

## TO SUM UP

A man of God, then, does not "suddenly appear." It takes time to become like Jesus Christ—a process, of course, that is not complete until we are with Him. But there is a definite level of spiritual maturity that is discernible, both by the individual who is evaluating his own life as well as those who associate with him. Otherwise, Paul would not have told Timothy and Titus to choose a certain kind of man. He was obviously recognizable.

"Where do I begin?" you ask. The answer is to take each of these characteristics, understand what it means, and then set up each one as a goal for your life. Then proceed moment by moment and day by day to become this kind of man.

**Footnotes**

1. As will be shown later, being "able to teach" does not seem to refer to the "gift of teaching" mentioned in Ephesians 4:11 and 1 Corinthians 12:28.
2. The New Testament writers use two words to describe the pastoral leaders in the local church—bishop and elder. These words are used interchangeably by several New Testament writers. For a fuller treatment why this is done, see Gene A. Getz, *Sharpening the Focus of the Church* (Chicago: Moody Press, 1973).

2

ABOVE REPROACH

*An overseer, then,*
*must be **above reproach** . . .*
*1 Timothy 3:2*

A man of God has a good reputation. This quality is listed in both the letter to Timothy (3:2) and the one to Titus (1:6,7). In fact, Paul mentions it twice in his letter to Titus.

As Paul wrote these letters, he was probably using this characteristic as an overarching one. It was his proposition, his summary idea, as it were, for all the qualities he was about to list. This quality as listed by Paul in this correspondence is not a new idea in the New Testament. In fact, when the church faced its first organizational problem in Jerusalem, the apostles recommended that seven men "of good reputation" be selected to help solve the problem of food distribution (Acts 6:3).

Later when Paul came to Lystra on his second missionary journey, he heard about Timothy. "He was well spoken of by the brethren who were in

Lystra and Iconium" (Acts 16:2). In other words, he had a *good reputation.*

Notice three things. First, people *were talking about* Timothy. A good reputation creates conversation—positive feedback.

Second, it was more than one person who was doing the talking. A good test of whether or not a person has a good reputation is *how many* people are talking. All of us have one or two prejudiced friends. But what are people in general saying? This is the true test.

And third, people were talking about him in both Lystra and Iconium, that is, in more than one location. Timothy's reputation was good *both* at home and abroad. When the two are in alignment, you can rest assured that you are getting a much clearer reading on a man's *inner* qualities. Paul was impressed with Timothy's reputation. This was the man he wanted "to go with him" (Acts 16:3).

It takes time to build a good reputation. But it should be a goal for every Christian, and your goal. In fact, it should happen naturally when a person is growing and maturing in his Christian life. Conversely, the Christian with a poor reputation is no doubt exhibiting traits that are not in harmony with Christian principles, nor are they in harmony with what people naturally expect from mature personalities.

## RECOGNIZING A MAN
## WITH A GOOD REPUTATION

When discussing this quality of a good reputation with a group of Christian men, I asked them what they thought of and what words they might use to describe a Christian man with a good reputation. Following are the results of our discussion:

He is a lovable guy!

He is honest; I'd trust him with
my bank account!

He is a sensitive person!

He radiates Christ!

He is a good father!

He loves people—his wife, his family,
everybody!

He works hard!

He sure is a humble guy!

He keeps his word!

He is not self-centered or conceited!

He makes you feel comfortable!

I can recommend him for most any task!

He doesn't let you down!

He won't take advantage of you!

He is not an opportunist!

He doesn't use people for his own ends!

He knows where he's going; he plans ahead!

He is thoughtful and cordial!

He is fair!

He is a good steward of time and talent!

He doesn't lose his cool!

He is consistent!

He recognizes and respects authority!

He hangs in there and perseveres!

He admits when he is wrong!

He is teachable!

He doesn't have a martyr complex!

He is an honest person!

You know what he is thinking!

But he is discretionary to *whom* he says what!

It is rather interesting that this list of comments that grew out of a brainstorming situation is in many ways remarkably similar to the list of qualifications that Paul listed in 1 Timothy 3 and Titus 1. This is probably not an accident, for if Paul summarized a man of God with the phrase "above reproach" and then filled in the details by listing the specific traits that create this situation, then it should not be too surprising that a spontaneous discussion of how to recognize a "good reputation" would produce a similar list of qualities to that of Paul's.

## A PERSONAL PROJECT

This personal project is designed to help you launch into this study and to begin to develop a good reputation.

## Step A

Honestly ask yourself what evidence you have that you have a good reputation. The following questions will help:

1. Do I get positive feedback from those *closest* to me that would indicate that I have a good reputation—from my wife, my children, my friends?

*Note:* Feedback from those who do not know you as well is not as good a test. Their judgments can be very superficial. They may be impressed with your physical appearance, or with your speaking ability, or with your "platform" personality, which may or may not represent what you *really* are as a person.

2. Do more and more people seek me out as a person and share their lives with me? Do people trust me with confidential information?

3. Do my relationships with people grow deeper and more significant the longer they know me and the closer they get to me? Or do my friendships grow strained and shallow as people learn to know what I am really like?

4. Does my circle of friends grow continually wider and larger? Is there an increasing number of people who admire and trust me?

5. Do people recommend me for significant or difficult tasks without fear of my letting them down?

## Step B

If you have difficulties in being objective about the answers to these questions, sit down with your spouse or a close friend and ask her/him to *honestly* help you evaluate the answers.

*Note:* If you take Step A and Step B, you will find it much easier to follow through in this study. You may find this project threatening, but remember it is your fear of what you might hear that will cause you to react negatively. Spiritual pride and bondage to self is a difficult hurdle; but, once you begin, you will be on your way to becoming a more mature man of God.

# HUSBAND OF ONE WIFE

*An overseer, then, must*
*be above reproach,*
**the husband of one wife** . . .
*1 Timothy 3:2*


This qualification for leadership has puzzled many people. There are a variety of interpretations of what Paul may mean, but the simplest interpretation seems to indicate that Paul is saying that a spiritual leader in the church must be intimately related to only one woman. But, if this be true, why would Paul have to mention such an obvious standard for acceptable Christian behavior? The answer to this question is not difficult when we consider the New Testament culture and its pagan practices and its lingering influence on people.

Look at the Corinthians! They were tolerating and even bragging about a man who was having a sexual relationship with his step-mother, an act of immorality that was not even practiced by the pagan community. The non-Christians in Corinth may have been licentious and immoral people, but they evidently didn't practice this kind of behavior (see 1 Cor. 5:1).

If a New Testament church tolerated this type of degeneracy, it is not surprising that Paul made sure that Christians knew that a man of God must be married to one woman and that he was to be loyal to her and to her alone.

Furthermore, consider the heart of man that is forever rationalizing regarding God's standards. Even Joseph Smith, in the nineteenth century, a leader and elder in a religious movement, contrived a way to make polygamy compatible with Christianity. And if it were not outlawed by the laws of the land, thousands of Mormons would no doubt be practicing this approach to marriage in direct violation of God's standard.

## A LARGER MEANING

But Christian morality extends its boundaries beyond the physical act of sexual intercourse. Jesus Christ Himself spoke directly to this issue: "You have heard that it was said, 'You shall not commit adultery', but I say unto you, that everyone who looks on a woman to lust for her has committed adultery with her already in his heart" (Matt. 5:27,28).

"To lust for her" means to desire greatly in a sexual, physical relationship. This differentiates *temptation* from *lust* or *sin*. Every red-blooded man—married or single—is tempted. No one can avoid completely the twentieth-century sensuous vibrations that emanate from magazine covers, movie ads, television commercials. Add to this the multitude of sensuously dressed women and female exhibitionists that permeate our culture, and it is not difficult to understand why many men are tempted every day of their lives. But to be tempted is not to sin. However, temptation can lead *to* sin. Any man who secretly and deliberately enjoys an illegitimate sexual relationship with a woman in his mind has, in God's sight, already committed an immoral act.

There is a fine line here, of course, which is not easy to describe for every individual. Men also differ in their sexual needs and drives. Some men are able to handle more provocative situations without too much difficulty. Others are extremely vulnerable to any circumstance that is sexually stimulating. Every Christian man must come to grips with his own inner struggles and concerns regarding moral purity. Far better to be too careful than to allow the subtle influence of the world to lead to mental adultery.

But there are some other facets to this problem that are very significant. Usually a happily married man (which includes a satisfactory sex life) can handle ordinary temptations quite well. Even pastors and other counselors can discuss problems with the opposite sex without losing objectivity and becoming indiscriminate and lustful. But a man who does not have a happy sex life must avoid counseling women like the plague. He is definitely flirting with danger. Temptation can very easily turn to lust and sin— either mentally or physically.

Single men, too, must be very careful. Fortunately, men who are married and who face daily sexual stimulation in the almost unavoidable realities of life have a natural and legitimate means for relieving the built-up sexual tensions that accompany temptation. But single men can find themselves fighting a severe and continuous battle with sexual desire, particularly if they are not discriminate in what they allow to come into their minds. There are sufficient situations that are unavoidable without deliberately aggravating the problem through careless actions.

## SOME PRACTICAL SUGGESTIONS

In my own study of this qualification with a group of Christian men, we discussed practical steps we could take to be men of high moral quality. Following are some of our conclusions:

1. We must develop good communications with our wives.

A married man who is able to keep his "moral house" in order and who is able to handle the normal temptations that arise in our contemporary culture must be a man who has a satisfactory sex life.

Paul speaks to this problem in 1 Corinthians 7:1-5. Here he instructs *both* wives and husbands to meet each other's sexual needs so that Satan does not lead one or the other into sexual immorality and unfaithfulness. Many a married man has gotten involved with another woman, either mentally or physically, because of a wife who is insensitive to his sexual and psychological needs. She may be selfish or even hostile, using sex as a weapon. Or she may just be naive and unaware of the tremendous drives that can be triggered in a red-blooded man who has faced temptation all day long in the office. But many men are also to blame here. They often suffer in silence and do not communicate to their wives, or they may sin against their wives and then blame them for not meeting their needs.

The average Christian woman may know very little of the inner problems of men—even *her* man. First, women cannot identify internally with the problem because they, by creation, do not function in their sex life physically or psychologically like a man. Second, if they are not instructed in the differences between the sexes, they may have no way of knowing how significant their role is in the sexual union. There *must* be communication if there is to be understanding and sensitivity.

2. We should not set up conflict situations by deliberately exposing ourselves to temptation.

Several of the men in our group travel extensively, and it was their consensus that airport newsstands are not conducive to moral purity. Most of these places of business specialize in pornography of all shades and varieties. It may be a "convenient" place for Christian men to catch up on what is happening in *Playboy* without buying a copy, but it can also inject a lot of carbon into a man's Christian life—calling for a very definite spiritual tune-up.

This is not to imply that it is impossible to scan pornography without sinning, but there are few men who, if honest, will not admit they are affected negatively by the exposure. There are some men who absolutely cannot do it without sinning.

In the provocative society in which we live and no matter what our spiritual maturity, we must guard against deliberately exposing ourselves to literature, movies, TV shows, and activities of any kind that are designed to illegitimately excite and stimulate a person's sexual nature.

This advice is even more significant for a single man. As stated before, a married man has a legitimate means—the marriage bed—for maintaining his sexual equilibrium. But a single man, once highly stimulated through improper exposure, finds himself in a desperate plight. There is only one answer to the single man's dilemma in our contemporary culture, that is, if he chooses to remain single. It's Paul's answer to young Timothy who also lived in a provocative society. He must "flee from youthful lust and pursue after righteousness" (2 Tim. 2:22).

3. We should fortify ourselves through regular study of the Word of God and prayer.

Nothing dulls a desire for communication with God and the study of His Word so much as indiscriminate exposure to illegitimate sexual stimuli. And nothing is so effective in combating temptation and lust as an effective prayer life and Bible study program. Thus, the apostle Paul wrote, "Whatever is true, whatever is honorable, whatever is right, whatever is pure, whatever is lovely, whatever is of good repute, if there is any excellence and if anything worthy of praise, let your mind dwell on these things" (Phil. 4:8).

4. We must avoid unnecessary idleness.

This was David's moral downfall! His temptation turned to lust and sin while he was busy doing nothing. When temptation is strong, idleness is pure folly. It has been the preliminary step to the downfall of many men, even spiritual leaders.

5. We should seek help from someone we can trust if the problem seems beyond our control.

If there is a lack of understanding and sensitivity and communication in your married life, perhaps you need someone else to help you. On occasions, I have seen the problem so severe that a husband is unable to verbalize his feelings directly to his wife. He has need of a third person: an understanding counselor or helper and interpreter.

Or perhaps, as a single man, you are fighting a losing battle with lust. Of all people, you need an understanding friend and helper—a prayer partner, a listener, an adviser. But by all means, don't do as I have seen some single men do, that is, share their problems with a single girl, or even a married woman. You need a mature man of God who can help you work through your problems.

## A PERSONAL PROJECT
The following personal projects are designed to help you maintain a life of moral purity.

### Step A
*For the Married Man:* Ask your wife to read this chapter on her own. State that your purpose is to form a common basis for discussion.

*For the Single Person:* List three of the greatest problems you face which are related to your sexual nature.

### Step B
*For the Married Man:* Discuss the chapter togeth-

er, using the following questions as guidelines:

1. How do you as a woman differ from me as a man, especially in your sexual feelings, needs, and attitudes?

2. How do you as a man differ from me as a woman, especially in your sexual feelings, needs, and attitudes?

3. What can each of us do—in our attitudes and behavior—to better meet each other's needs sexually?

*For the Single Person:* Study these problems carefully and then honestly answer the following questions:

1. What am I doing to accentuate these problems?

2. What can I do on my own to solve these problems?

3. Can I solve all of these problems alone, or do I need help from a trustworthy friend or competent counselor?

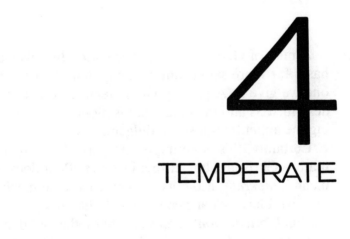

# 4
## TEMPERATE

*An overseer, then,*
*must be above reproach,*
*the husband of one wife,*
***temperate*** . . .
*1 Timothy 3:2*

A man of God should be *temperate*. But this word has a far more significant meaning than the ordinary one we give it. A person who is temperate is usually described as an individual who is moderate in indulging the appetite; not self-indulgent.

Certainly, this is an important part of becoming a mature Christian, but in this instance, Paul does not mean *temperate* in the usual sense. Here he means a man who has a clear *perspective* on life and a correct spiritual *orientation*. Thayer defines the word as a state untouched by any slumberous or beclouding influence. Put another way, a man who is temperate does not lose his physical, psychological, and spiritual orientation. He remains stable and steadfast, and his thinking is clear. Put in more relevant terms, he is "calm, cool and collected" in most situations. Most of all, he doesn't lose perspective because of false security.

Paul uses this same word in 1 Thessalonians, chapter 5, in talking about the coming day of judgment (5:2,3). We are not to "sleep as others do" but we are to be "alert and sober (temperate)" (5:6).

There are those who talk about "peace and safety," that all is going well, and there is nothing to fear. Man is in control! Human genius will solve our problems and keep us safe and free from danger! Population, pollution, and the threat of nuclear war, why worry? Man can handle these problems. But, while all of this is happening—"While they are saying, 'Peace and safety!' then destruction will come upon them suddenly like birthpains upon a woman with child, and they shall not escape" (5:3).

A mature Christian man has a correct view regarding the "temporariness" of this life and everything in it. He does not allow himself to get caught up in the "false security" of what appears to be human progress. He walks in the "light" of the Word of God and not in the "darkness" of the word of man (5:4,5).

Paul goes on in this Thessalonian passage to tell us how to develop this quality of life; how to become temperate in the midst of subtle human progress. "Let us be sober [temperate]," says Paul, "having put on the breastplate of faith and love, and as a helmet, the hope of salvation" (5:8). Anyone familiar with the Pauline correspondence knows that *faith, hope, and love* are three key words he uses frequently to measure the maturity level of the body of Jesus

Christ. When writing to churches he was truly proud of, he would often thank God for their faith, their hope and their love (Col. 1:3-5; Eph. 1:15-18; 1 Thess. 1:2,3; 2 Thess. 1:3,4).

## A MAN OF FAITH

A man of God, the *temperate* man, is a *man of faith*. Like men of old—Abel, Noah, Abraham, Isaac, and Moses—and others who are catalogued so dramatically in Hebrews 11, a mature man of God steps out and acts on the promises of God.

Notice the "faith *and* action" of each of these men:

1. By faith Abel *offered* a better sacrifice than Cain (11:4)
2. By faith, Noah *prepared* an ark (11:7)
3. By faith, Abraham *obeyed by going out* (11:8)
4. By faith, Abraham *offered up* Isaac (11:17)
5. By faith, Isaac *blessed* Jacob (11:20)
6. By faith, Moses *left* Egypt (11:23)

All of these Old Testament men listed above "died in faith, without receiving the promises, but having seen them and having followed them from a distance, and having confessed that they were strangers and exiles on earth" (Heb. 11:13).

Today, a man of God, a temperate man, *believes* God and *acts* on His promises even though he does not understand totally what lies ahead. And even if the present world and the progress of men seems to indicate that "all is well" and that peace is here, a *temperate* man knows that it will not continue and that the world is headed towards ultimate destruc-

40

tion. By faith, he keeps looking for the second coming of Jesus Christ to deliver him from the wrath to come (1 Thess. 5:9). Furthermore, he encourages other believers with this truth and helps build up all members of the body of Christ, helping them to look forward to that day (5:11). By word and example, he holds forth the exhortation given in Hebrews 12:1,2: "Let us also lay aside every encumbrance, and the sin which so easily entangles us, and let us run with endurance the race that is set before us, fixing our eyes on Jesus the author and perfecter of faith."

## A MAN OF HOPE

Closely aligned with the quality of *faith* is that of *hope* which refers to both the *object* of our faith as well as our *present attitude* and *state of being* (Heb. 11:1).

Hope as the object of our faith refers to our eternal inheritance (1 Pet. 1:3,4). Our hope is laid up for us in heaven (Col. 1:5). It is the "hope of salvation" (1 Thess. 5:8). It is "the hope of eternal life, which God, who cannot lie, promised long ages ago" (Titus 1:2) that will all be culminated with our "blessed hope and appearing of the glory of our great God and Saviour, Christ Jesus" (Titus 2:13).

But hope is also described as a present state of being. A man of hope is *steadfast* (1 Thess. 1:3). He has *fixed* his hope "on the living God" (1 Tim. 4:10), rather than on the "uncertainty of riches" and the things of this world (1 Tim. 6:17). He *holds fast* the confession of his hope "without wavering" (Heb.

10:23), and has *fixed* his "hope completely on the grace to be brought . . . at the revelation of Jesus Christ" (1 Pet. 1:13).

In summary, a *temperate man* is a man of hope. And a *man of hope* is a mature, stable man because he is sure of his future state-of-being. Present circumstances do not give him false security, nor do they create insecurity. His past, present and future perspectives are clear, sharp, and theologically correct.

## A MAN OF LOVE

A temperate man is also a man of love (1 Thess. 5:8). This, Paul says, is the greatest thing—the most important of all these qualities. "But now abide faith, hope, love, these three; but the greatest of these is love" (1 Cor. 13:13).

And, continues the apostle, "Love is patient, love is kind and is not jealous; love does not brag and is not arrogant; does not act unbecomingly; it does not seek its own, does not provoke, does not take into account the wrong suffered, does not rejoice in unrighteousness, but rejoices with the truth" (1 Cor. 13:4-6).

Henry Drummond classifies this paragraph as the spectrum of love—nine ingredients that must be present for true love to exist:

Patience — kindness — generosity — humility — courtesy — unselfishness — good temper — guilelessness — sincerity.

And why is love the greatest thing? Because, says Paul, it "bears all things, believes all things, hopes all things, endures all things" (13:7).

Love, then, is really foundational to *faith,* for love "believes all things." It is also foundational to hope, for love "hopes all things." And furthermore, love is the greatest, because it "never fails" (13:8).

Faith, hope, and love then are foundational to having a clear perspective on life. "Since we are of the day," wrote Paul, "let us be sober (temperate), having on the breastplate of faith and love, and as a helmet, the hope of salvation" (1 Thess. 5:8).

## A PERSONAL PROJECT
This personal project is designed to help you develop the quality of temperance.

### Step A
Answer the following questions as honestly as you can:

1. How strong is my faith in God and His Word? Do I *really* believe He exists and that Jesus Christ is coming again? If I do, how is my faith revealed in my *actions*?

2. How much aware am I of the "hope of my calling?" (Eph. 1:18). How fully do I understand "the riches of the glory of His inheritance in the saints, and what is the surpassing greatness of His power toward us who believe"? (Eph. 1:18,19). Have I fixed my hope on the things of this world, or on eternal values? (See Matt. 6:33.)

3. Am I a man of love? How well do I measure up to the criteria prescribed in 1 Corinthians 13? Am I patient? Am I kind? Am I generous? Am I humble?

43

Am I courteous? Am I unselfish? Am I controlled?
Am I pure in motives? Am I sincere?

## Step B

Proceed to develop your *faith, hope* and *love*. The
following ideas were generated by a group of Christian men as we first studied these characteristics together. Apply them in your own life.

1. Verbalize praise and thanksgiving to God for
loving and saving us.

2. Learn to claim the promises of God's Word.

3. Engage in personal Bible study and prayer. Remember that "faith comes from hearing, and hearing
by the Word of Christ" (Rom. 10:17).

4. Confer and share with mature Christians. Seek
help from the body of Christ.

5. Read biographies of great Christians.

6. In times of conflict, learn to submit and ask
God what He is trying to teach you.

7. Learn to set biblical priorities.

8. Learn to discern what is temporal and what is
eternal.

9. Realize that the physical body must have rest
and food and relaxation. Remember that it is easy to
lose perspective when we are mentally and emotionally exhausted. (Read the story of Elijah in 1 Kings
18:1—19:8. Note particularly Elijah's loss of perspective in 19:1-4. Notice also God's solution in
19:5-8.)

5
PRUDENT

*An overseer, then,*
*must be above reproach,*
*the husband of one wife,*
*temperate, **prudent** . . .*
*1 Timothy 3:2, Titus 1:8*

The word and its different forms which Paul uses to describe this mark of maturity (*sophron*) is variously translated as sober, sober-minded, sensible, of sound mind and judgment, or *prudent*.

Perhaps the best contextual commentary on what Paul had in mind is found in Romans 12:3. "For through the grace given to me I say to every man among you not to think more highly of himself than he ought to think; but to think so as to have sound judgment [that is, to think soberly, sensibly, or prudently], as God has allotted to each man a measure of faith."

Paul's thrust in this passage is to instruct Christians to have a proper view of themselves in relationship to God and to other Christians (Rom. 12:4-8). Evidently there were believers in Rome, as there were in Corinth (1 Cor. 12:14-27), who had an overly exalted view of their position in the body of Christ. Some no doubt felt they were God's "special gift" to the church. Consequently, Paul had to exhort them to be "devoted to one another in brotherly love" and to "give preference to one another in honor," rather than putting each other down (Rom. 12:10).

More than any other characteristic of maturity, Paul relates this concept specifically and deliberately to all members of the body of Christ. Within a span of five verses in Titus 2, he exhorts older men to be prudent or sensible (2:2), older women are to teach younger women to be prudent (2:4,5), and younger men likewise were to be prudent (2:6).[1]


## PRUDENCE—HOW CAN IT BE RECOGNIZED?

A prudent man is truly a *humble man*. He has a proper view of himself, and he is keenly aware of one thing: all that he has (gifts, ability, and possessions, etc.) are from God. Without Him, he is nothing at all.

A prudent man also has *a proper view of the grace of God*. He realizes that he was lost without Christ and that all of his human abilities and achievements were useless in winning any favor with God. He realizes that God in His boundless love sent His Son to die for lost humanity, "even while we were yet sinners" (Rom. 5:8). This was Paul's attitude regarding his own human inheritance and accomplishments.

Though he was "circumcized the eighth day," though he was "of the nation of Israel," and even "of the tribe of Benjamin," and not only "a Hebrew of the Hebrews," but also "a Pharisee," yet all of these he "counted as loss for the sake of Christ" (Phil. 3:4-7).

Paul never got over God's grace in calling him and redeeming him, even when he was going about persecuting other Christians. How *could* he think more highly of himself than he ought to think? A prudent man is *taught by that grace!* "For," said Paul, "the grace of God has appeared bringing salvation to all men, instructing us to deny ungodliness and worldly desires, and to live sensibly (or prudently), righteously and godly in the present age . . ." (Titus 2:11,12).

A true view of God's grace sends a man to his knees in humble and prayerful adoration, and then enables that man to rise to a new level of righteous and godly living. And speaking of prayer, *it is only the prudent man who can pray right.* Peter exhorts: "Be of sound judgment (be prudent) and sober spirit for the purpose of prayer" (1 Pet. 4:7). An attitude of pride leads to bad judgment and immature thinking even in our prayer life.


## AN IMPORTANT BALANCE

Before leaving this mark of maturity, it is important to note that prudence should not lead to weakness. To have a correct perspective on our place in God's family does not mean that we are to be withdrawn and inhibited. It does not mean a lack of self-confidence and a sense of worthlessness. Timothy, no doubt, had a problem in this area. Obviously he was being intimidated by those who opposed the work of God. Paul charged him to "not be ashamed" of the Lord or of Paul himself (2 Tim. 1:8). "For God," said Paul, "has not given us a spirit of timidity, but of power and love and discipline (that is, of a sound mind)" (2 Tim. 1:7).

A Christian should never be ashamed or inhibited. True humility is not weakness. A prudent man is one who recognizes his unworthiness to be called a child of God and to be a member of the family of God, but yet stands straight, with shoulders back and head held high. He has achieved that divine balance in his life between being a man whose gifts and abilities God can use and a man who gives all glory and honor to Jesus Christ. Paul himself did not hesitate to commend himself when falsely accused and belittled. But he made sure that his motives were understood—that he was doing so because of what God had done in *his* life.

In writing to the Corinthians and defending his apostleship against those who falsely questioned his motives, he said: "For if we are beside ourselves, it is for God; if we are of sound mind (prudent) it is for you" (2 Cor. 5:13). In other words, said Paul, you may think we are bragging and are proud. If so, it is because of what God has wrought in us. We are only glorifying the work of God in our lives. And from your viewpoint, Corinthians, we want you to see us as sober, prudent and sensible men, humbly acknowledging that we are what we are because of God's marvelous grace (cf. 2 Cor. 11—12).

## A PERSONAL PROJECT

The following personal project is designed to help you become a prudent person. This means becoming wise and balanced in judgment. And more specifically, it means that you must develop a proper self-image.

Christians frequently go to two extremes. Either they see themselves as *nothing* or they are caught up with an *exalted* view of themselves. An immature person finds himself vacillating between these two attitudes.

Actually both approaches are improper. Christians, of all people, should be balanced in this area of their life. On the one hand, we must recognize that all we are and have is because of God's grace. On the other hand, we must recognize that we have not only human but divine resources to do great exploits for God.

How do we develop a "sound mind" enabling us to maintain this balance?

## Step A

Recognize that there are reasons for this problem to exist and persist. The following check list will help you to begin to isolate the source of your problem.

1. An unfortunate series of circumstances beyond human control.

☐ Such as loss of a parent or parents.

☐ Bad experiences in school or in the neighborhood.

☐ Bad influences from others.

☐ Hereditary factors or physical illness creating feelings of inferiority.

2. An incorrect theology.

☐ Such as being taught so long you are "nothing," that you actually feel and believe you are "nothing."

☐ Such as trying so hard to "crucify self" that you have downgraded your "self-image" and the "image of God" in you.

☐ Such as an incorrect view of forgiveness and being right with God; that is, trying to become "nothing" before God accepts you.

*Remember:* You cannot do anything to become right with God. You cannot even become "nothing." You must come to God just as you are and accept His free gift of salvation.

3. Parents who were unwise in rearing me.

☐ Either they withheld praise and attention, creating in me an unnatural thirst and desire for recognition.

☐ Or they were unwise in giving me too much of a prominent position, creating an emotional need to always be "first in line" and in the "limelight."

*Note:* The first situation (a) is far more prevalent than the second situation (b). Christian parents especially, often withhold praise and attention from their children for fear they will create pride. Actually they achieve what they are trying to avoid. They create a person who is starved for attention, and one who has a tremendous pride problem later in life because he cannot handle success, emotionally.

## Step B

Now that you have isolated your problem, interact

51

with someone you trust—someone who is wise and *prudent*. Ask that person to help you develop perspective and to pray with you about your problem.

## Step C

Set up specific goals for your life in this area.

*Warning:* Do not become guilty of rationalizing immature behavior on the basis of past circumstances. Become a responsible person. Don't blame your problems on someone else, even though they may have contributed to the problem.

## Step D

Ask God to help you overcome your problem. Remember the Word of God which says, "And if any of you lack wisdom, let him ask of God who gives to all men generously and without reproach and it shall be given to him" (Jas. 1:5).

### Footnotes

1. Note Paul's special application of the word "prudent" to women in 1 Timothy 2:9,15. Here this characteristic is related to the way she adorns herself. She is to adorn herself "with proper clothing, modestly and DISCREETLY (prudently), not with braided hair and gold or pearls or costly garments" (1 Tim. 2:9). Paul, of course, is not saying women should not be attractive; rather he is exhorting them to be truly humble and to keep their motives pure, not attracting attention to themselves merely through external means. They are not to desire a place of prominence in the church, but rather to "quietly receive instructions with entire submissiveness" (2:11). And it is with this attitude she will truly find freedom and fulfillment in the Christian life (2:15).

6

RESPECTABLE

*An overseer, then,*
*must be above reproach,*
*the husband of one wife,*
*temperate, prudent,*
**respectable** . . .
*1 Timothy 3:2*

A certain man and his wife in a certain city bought a home and moved in. This man was a Christian and the man from whom he purchased the house was also a Christian. In fact, both were Christian Ministers.

In a few short days, it became quite apparent that certain of the neighbors were quite disturbed that another minister had moved next door. For behold, the former minister had paid little attention to the outward appearance of his property. He allowed the grass to grow long and *when* he did mow it, certain sections were left uncut, and *where* he mowed, mounds of dry grass accumulated, making a shabby appearance. Dandelions grew rampant, and other assorted weeds became a permanent part of the landscape. He planted no trees or shrubs, but allowed his large and spacious lawn to become a hayfield.

It just so happened that certain of the neighbors in this particular community paid special attention to the outward appearance of their homes. True, they were not Christians (the majority), and they were quite materialistic. Their houses and their lawns even appeared to be their "god."

But they were totally turned off by this minister's irresponsibility and lack of orderliness and unwillingness to do his part to add to the natural beauty of the neighborhood. Consequently the Christian man moving in after the former man moved away, found great communication barriers with his non-Christian neighbors. They were utterly convinced that Christians (ministers particularly) are a bad lot—that they are really quite disorderly and unconcerned about outward beauty and decor.

## THE INTERPRETATION

This twentieth century parable is true! It happened to me. I was the man who moved in and faced the communication barriers. And I share it with you now because it illustrates how a man can be a Christian—even a Christian minister—and not measure up to the qualification of being *respectable*.

The word *kosmios*, translated in 1 Timothy 3:2 as being "of good behavior," "well behaved," or "respectable," actually means orderly or well-arranged. Thus, it is speaking here of a man who is living a well-ordered life.

Paul also uses the word to describe the way a woman should dress (1 Tim. 2:9). Her clothing should be proper or becoming and modest. What she puts on, the jewelry she wears, the way she fixes her hair are all to be appropriate to a woman "making a claim to godliness" (1 Tim. 2:10).

Many Christian women (and men), of course, misinterpret what Paul is saying. They go to the other extreme and appear drab and dowdy. They miss the whole spirit of Paul's concern which is inner beauty and motives. He is admonishing the woman who attempts to attract attention to herself—not to the Lord—by means of outward decoration and adornment. It is only the external and superficial which is visible. This, says Paul, is not calling attention to Jesus Christ but rather to one's self. This is not orderly or respectable behavior.

By contrast a person who is unattractive externally also calls attention to himself and presents an image of Jesus Christ as one of being backward, uncultured, and "peculiar" in the bad sense of that word. In short, they also are not *respectable*.

The verb form of this word is even more enlightening (*kosmeo*). It is used by our Lord to describe a "well-ordered" house (Matt. 12:44), "decorated" tombstones (Matt. 23:29), and "well-trimmed" lamps (Matt. 25:7). And Jesus Christ also talked about the Temple that "was adorned with beautiful stones and votive gifts" (Luke 21:5).

But perhaps the most powerful use of this word appears in Paul's letter to Titus when he urges slaves to "be subject to their own masters in everything." They are to be "well pleasing, not argumentative," and they are not to steal from their masters. Rather they are to "*adorn* the doctrine of God our Saviour in every respect" (Titus 2:9,10). This illustration, of course, broadens the concept of *respectability* tremendously. No matter what our position or profession, we are to live in such a way that our lives are becoming to the teachings of the Word of God. Specifically, Paul here treats obedience to those in authority having a non-argumentative and honest relationship with people. To violate these New Testament teachings is to violate the quality of being respectable.

Paul is saying that a man who is respectable is a man who lives in such a way that his life-style adorns the teachings of the Bible. Whether it be his dress, his speech, the appearance of his home, his office, or the way he does business—all are to be in proper relationship to biblical principles and doctrines. Since God is a God of order, a man of God too should be orderly and proper. He is to be a Christian gentleman in all areas of his life.

## A PERSONAL PROJECT

This personal project is designed to help you develop the quality of respectability.

### Step A

Evaluate your life-style openly and honestly before God. The following questions will help you.

1. What about my external appearance? Does it measure up to what is considered proper both biblically and culturally?

*Note:* It is important to keep these two in balance. Usually, but not always, the culture itself makes certain demands on people. Even the non-Christian has certain expectations regarding what is appropriate and what is inappropriate. It is important for a Christian to take into consideration cultural expectations and at the same time not to violate biblical principles and teachings.

2. What are my motives in relationship to what I wear? Am I merely attracting attention to myself or to the Lord Jesus Christ who lives within me?

*Note:* This can go to two extremes. Either I can dress elaborately in order to attract attention to myself, or I can be shabby, unkempt, or even unclean in order to attract attention to myself. Both lead to a lack of respectability.

3. What about the house I live in? Did I buy it to impress people, or did I buy it to glorify Jesus Christ?

*Note:* This question, as all of these questions, have to be handled individually. Size, cost and location are not the most important issues; however, your *motives* are!

4. What about my speech? Do I use words to build up others or to build up myself. Do I glorify God with my words, or do I glorify myself? And furthermore is my speech becoming to a Christian? Does it adorn the doctrine of God?

5. What about my life-style in general? Does it reflect the life-style of Jesus Christ?

## Step B

Consider these scriptural admonitions. Use them as a check list. Are they true in your life? To put them into practice will help you to become a respectable person both among Christians and non-Christians. Check those areas where you feel you are particularly weak.

**BUSINESS LIFE**

☐ "But we urge you, brethren, to excel still more, and to make it your ambition to lead a quiet life and attend to your own business and work with your own hands, just as we commanded you; so that you may behave properly toward outsiders and may not be in any need" (1 Thess. 4:10-12).

☐ "Whatever you do, do your work heartily, as for the Lord rather than for men; knowing that from the Lord you will receive the reward of the inheritance. It is the Lord Christ whom you serve" (Col. 3:23,24).

☐ "And let those who have believers as their masters not be disrespectful to them because they are brethren, but let them serve them all the more, because those who partake of the benefit are believers and beloved" (1 Tim. 6:2).

**SOCIAL LIFE**

☐ "Whether, then, you eat or drink or whatever you do, do all to the glory of God. Give no offense either to Jews or to Greeks or to the church of God; just as I also please all men in all things, not seeking my own profit, but the profit of the many, that they may be saved" (1 Cor. 10:31-33).

☐ "Conduct yourselves with wisdom toward outsiders, making the most of the opportunity. Let your speech always be with grace, seasoned, as it were, with salt, so that you may know how you may respond to each person" (Col. 4:5,6).

☐ Keep your behavior excellent among the Gentiles, so that in the thing in which they slander you as evildoers, they may on account of your good deeds, as they observe them, glorify God in the day of visitation" (1 Pet. 2:12).

☐ "Submit yourselves for the Lord's sake to every human institution, whether to a king as the one in authority, or to governors as sent by him for the punishment of evildoers and the praise of those who do right. For such is the will of God that by doing right you may silence the ignorance of foolish men" (1 Pet. 2:13-15).

### CHURCH LIFE

☐ "Only conduct yourselves in a manner worthy of the gospel of Christ; so that whether I come and see you or remain absent, I may hear of you that are standing firm in one spirit, with one mind striving together for the faith of the gospel" (Phil. 1:27).

☐ "So then let us pursue the things which make for peace in the building up of one another" (Rom. 14:19).

☐ "Do nothing from selfishness or empty conceit, but with humility of mind, let each of you regard one another as more important than himself; do not merely look out for your own personal interests, but also for the interests of others" (Phil. 2:3,4).

☐ "But as for you, speak the things which are fitting for sound doctrine" (Titus 2:1).

## Step C

From this study, isolate areas of weakness in your own life. Set up these areas as goals for your life.

Proceed to reach these goals through prayer and deliberate action.

For example, if you are a person who never gets to work on time, make it a goal to get an early start and to be there early. Concentrate on this goal until you have developed a new habit.

*Note:* Prayer alone will not achieve this goal. You must act as a *responsible* human being. You must put feet to your prayers.

*Remember:* Bad habits are hard to break, but we *must* break them if we are to become respectable—that is, more and more like Jesus Christ.

# 7

HOSPITABLE

*An overseer, then,*
*must be above reproach,*
*the husband of one wife,*
*temperate, prudent,*
*respectable, **hospitable** . . .*
*1 Timothy 3:2; Titus 1:8*


Hospitality is not a new concept. It is not even distinctive to Christianity. It has been a part of oriental culture for a long time, and even considered a sacred responsibility. The Greeks considered hospitality a religious duty, and of course, God gave specific instructions to the children of Israel; so specific no man could plead ignorance: "When a stranger resides with you in your land, you shall not do him wrong. The stranger who resides with you shall be to you as the native among you, and you shall love him as yourself . . ." (Lev. 19:33,34).

Merrill Unger reminds us that even today among the Arabs, we can see a reflection of this ancient custom: "A traveler may sit at the door of a perfect stranger and smoke a pipe until the master welcomes him with an evening meal and then tarry a limited number of days without inquiry as to his purposes, and depart with a simple 'God be with you' as his only compensation."[1]

## CHRISTIAN HOSPITALITY

What was instituted by God in the Old Testament is reconfirmed in the New, and given even a greater dimension. Christians, of all people, are to be hospitable. It is truly a mark of Christian maturity. It is not to be just a sacred responsibility or religious duty, but rather an act of *Christian love.* It is this love that provides the basic motivation for reaching out to others.

Christian hospitality is to operate in a context of love. It is clear from the context of Scripture. Paul wrote to the Romans: 'Let love be without hypocrisy" (12:9); "Be devoted to one another in brotherly love" (12:10). And then Paul culminates these potent directives with another: "Practice hospitality" (12:13).

Notice also Hebrews 13:1,2: "Let love of the brethren continue. Do not neglect to show hospitality to strangers . . ."

Peter, too, ties hospitality in with the concept of love. "Above all, keep fervent in your love for one another, because love covers a multitude of sins" (1 Pet. 4:8). And then he follows this admonition immediately by saying: "Be hospitable to one another without complaint" (4:9). "Without complaint." Here is the true test of Christian love. Mere responsibility or duty may lead to performance but not from the heart. Christians are to love others—not for reward—but because God first loved us. There will, of course, be reward. You cannot truly reach out to others without eventually receiving. But "receiving" is not to be a part of our basic motive in Christian love and hospitality.

Saint Francis of Assisi put it well in his classic prayer:

"Lord, make me an instrument of your peace;
where there is hatred, let me sow love;
where there is injury, pardon;
where there is doubt, faith;
where there is despair, hope;
where there is darkness, light;
where there is sadness, joy.

O Divine Master, grant that I may not so
    much seek
to be consoled as to console;
to be understood as to understand;
to be loved as to love;
for it is in giving that we receive,
it is in pardoning that we are pardoned,
it is in dying that we are born to
    eternal life."

## THE CONTEXT OF HOSPITALITY

It is already clear from the Scriptures just cited that Christian hospitality, first of all, is to be demonstrated toward other Christians. But it is also obvious that Christians are to be hospitable towards *all* men. On several occasions New Testament writers quote

God's commandments to Israel, which was stated by Moses when instructing them regarding showing hospitality toward strangers and aliens (Lev. 19:34): "You shall love your neighbor as yourself," says Paul to the Romans (13:9). And to the Galatians he wrote: "For the whole law is fulfilled in one word, in the statement, 'you shall love your neighbor as yourself' " (Gal. 5:14).

James gives a larger perspective and helps us understand who our neighbor is (Jas. 2:6-9). It is the *poor man* as well as the *rich!* We must not show partiality. This is sin.

The Scriptures make it clear. We must love all men—regardless of race, color, or creed. To do less is to violate the law of love instituted by Jesus Christ Himself. Jesus reminds us that this law is also the Christian's bridge to the world. "By this," He said, "all men will know that you are My disciples, if you have love for one another" (John 13:35).

## HOSPITALITY AND CULTURE

Cultures vary and so do human needs. The society in which New Testament Christians lived was certainly much different from our twentieth-century Western culture. In fact, we see variations within the New Testament culture, depending on geographical locations. We even see changes taking place within specific locations. For example, there were hospitality needs in Jerusalem during the early days of the church which led to a temporary communal system (Acts 2:42-47). Later a famine hit the New Testament world, evidently creating particular needs

among the Christians in Judea. Christians met this
need (Acts 11:29).

But as needs changed, so did the church in trying
to meet these needs in a specific way. "To show hospitality" is a supra-cultural absolute. Christians have
no choice; that is, if they want to be doing God's will.
But how it is done is related to the specific needs at
any given moment in history and at any given geographical location.

## A MARK OF CHRISTIAN MATURITY

Paul says that *hospitality* is a mark of Christian
maturity. And it is specifically related to the man
who desires to be a spiritual leader in the church.
Obviously, Paul is referring primarily to *how* a man
uses his home. In other words, it is a mark of *personal
maturity*. The characteristic of hospitality, of course,
*needs* to be individualized (as Paul illustrates in
1 Tim. 3:2), but it cannot be seen in isolation. It is
also clear that Paul is implying that this mark of
maturity should be instilled in a man's whole family.
So it is also a mark of a *mature Christian home*.

But the context of hospitality is even broader. It is
also a mark of a *mature church*. No individual person or family can always meet the needs of others.
There are times when every member of the body of
Christ must join hands in showing hospitality.

## A PERSONAL PROJECT

This personal project is designed to help you develop the quality of hospitality.

## Step A

You must come to grips with that which is basic to Christian hospitality—love. You have already been introduced to this biblical concept. At this point you need to review. Do you really love others? Restudy the profile of biblical love in 1 Corinthians 13:4-7. Without love you cannot possibly show hospitality, at least in a Christian way.

*Warning:* Biblical love is not a feeling! It is an attitude and involves action. Christian love is patience, kindness, generosity, humility, courtesy, unselfishness, good temper, guilelessness, and sincerity. This is what Paul tells us in 1 Corinthians 13.

Therefore, do not *wait* for a desire to show hospitality. It may never come. You may need to start showing hospitality before you begin to sense reward at the *feeling* level. In fact, being hospitable may even threaten you. But remember, "perfect love casts out fear" (1 John 4:18). As you begin to practice biblical love, it is more and more perfected and matured, and fear and threat will subside.

## Step B

Decide on some specific ways to show hospitality—first to members of the body of Christ, and second to non-Christians. The following suggestions will help you:

1. Look for opportunities to share your home with spiritual leaders—pastors, missionaries, and other Christian workers. Invite them to dinner or to stay in your home.

*Warning:* There are religious hustlers, even among so-called evangelical Christians, but they are few.

And they can usually be spotted and should be dealt with in Christian love.

Paul sets a great example for Christian workers. Though he makes it very clear that a laborer is worthy of his hire, he himself bent over backwards not to take advantage of others financially or in any other way (1 Thess. 2:5-9).

2. Look for opportunities to share your home with other members of the body of Christ who compose your own local church. Remember, there doesn't have to be any special physical need to show hospitality. Perhaps the need is social and emotional and spiritual. Many Christians are lonely and in need of fellowship, and may be too bashful to reach out to others. They are waiting for an invitation to share their lives with someone else.

*Challenge:* If *you* are bashful and reserved, waiting for an invitation and then you criticize others for being unfriendly, reach out to others, even though you are afraid. You will be surprised how quickly others will respond to you. And it will be "in giving" that you will begin "to receive."

3. Begin to show hospitality to non-Christians by beginning with the people all around you—your neighbor across the street, or the person who works beside you at your job. Remember, *you* are the Christian; *you* are the one who should be reaching out. Invite them to dinner, or ask them to join you in an evening of relaxation and social activity.

*Note:* Don't get overly ambitious. Begin by building deep friendships with one or two non-Christians. Frequently this sets the stage for an invitation to a

Bible class in your home, or a personal witness for Jesus Christ.

4. Open your home for an informal Bible study, either for Christians or non-Christians. Strive to do both over a period of time.

*Remember:* To invite non-Christians to your home for a Bible study means building friendships first. You must learn to love people because they are people and not just because you want to win them to Christ.

## Step C

Now that you have an overview, set up some specific hospitality goals. For example, you might plan to invite a Christian couple to your home for dinner. *And* you might plan to invite your neighbor to join you for a picnic dinner in your backyard.

These goals are simple. But when you have achieved them, then proceed to develop additional goals that are more extensive and long range.

---

**Footnotes**

1. Merrill F. Unger, *Unger's Bible Dictionary* (Chicago: Moody Press, 1967), p. 502.

# 8

# ABLE TO TEACH

*An overseer, then,*
*must be above reproach,*
*the husband of one wife,*
*temperate, prudent,*
*respectable, hospitable,*
**able to teach** . . .
*1 Timothy 3:2; Titus 1:9*

This little phrase, "able to teach," is a fascinating concept. It comes from one word (in the Greek, *didaktikos*) and, though there are hundreds of references in the New Testament to some form of the word having to do with "teaching," this particular word is used only twice (1 Tim. 3:2; 2 Tim. 2:24)

Our tendency is to see this phrase, "able to teach," through our own psychological grid. We tend to think of "good teachers" we know—people who are effective communicators, able to use skillful methods and able to motivate people to learn. We may think of high-powered lecturers, individuals who can hold an audience spellbound for an hour. We think of ability and skill and expertise.

Actually these reflections seem to be quite indirectly related, and in some instances totally unrelated, to what Paul had in mind when he wrote to Timothy. There is a far more foundational meaning, and a profound meaning.

But before we look at what "able to teach" really means, there is another point that needs clarification. Neither does Paul seem to be referring to what the Bible classifies as the "gift of teaching." The New Testament records that this gift was given to only certain people (Eph. 4:11; 1 Cor. 12:28,29), whereas being "able to teach" is a *quality* that every man and woman can develop, and *must* develop to be mature.


## A QUALITY OF LIFE

Some feel this word should actually be translated "teachable," because of its root meanings and use in classical Greek. If so, all the more profound, for this truly refers to a quality of life—a person who is humble, sensitive, and desirous to know the will of God.

Actually this meaning is probably inherent in Paul's use of the word. But his use of the word in a larger context than 1 Timothy 3:2 appears to give it a much broader meaning. Look first at 2 Timothy 2:24. Notice the cluster of words and concepts surrounding "able to teach":

"But refuse foolish and ignorant speculations, knowing that they produce quarrels. And the Lord's bond-servant must not be quarrelsome, but be kind to all, able to teach, patient when wronged, with gentleness correcting those who are in opposition; if perhaps God may grant them repentance leading to the knowledge of the truth, and they may come to their senses and escape from the snare of the devil, having been held captive by him to do his will" (2 Tim. 2:23-26).

Here "able to teach" is surrounded by significant words, all having to do with *qualities* of life—qualities definitely related to the same characteristics listed in 1 Timothy 3 and Titus 1.

*Note:* Timothy was to *avoid quarrels.* He was to be *kind* to all people (Christians and non-Christians). He was to be *patient* when falsely accused and personally attacked. He was to correct those opposing him in a *gentle* manner. And sandwiched right in the middle of these qualities describing a mature person who is in control of himself is the phrase, *able to teach.*

It appears to be obvious! To be "able to teach" means that a man must possess certain personal qualities that enable him to communicate with others in a non-threatened, objective manner. He isn't the kind of person who goes around looking for arguments and actually stirring them up. He is sensitive to people, even those who are confused and even obstinate and bitter. When verbally, or even physically, attacked, he does not reciprocate with cutting words and "put downs," or *knockdowns.* In short, he is a man who is not in bondage to himself. He is secure as a person and is in control of his personality.

## A BASIC ATTITUDE TOWARD SCRIPTURE
But there appears to be another significant dimen-

sion to the meaning of being "able to teach." Though the basic word used in 1 Timothy 3:2 is not mentioned in Titus 1, Paul makes several statements that obviously refer to being "able to teach." The spiritual leader must be ". . . self-controlled, holding fast the faithful word which is in accordance with the teaching, that he may be able both to exhort in sound doctrine and to refute those who contradict" (Titus 1:8,9).

Notice that a man who is able to "exhort in sound doctrine and to refute those who contradict" must be a man who is "self-controlled." Here we have the same contextual meaning as in 2 Timothy 2:23-26.

Notice also that a man who is "able to teach" is a man who has certain convictions regarding the Word of God. He is "holding fast" the faithful Word! He is not given over to "foolish and ignorant speculation"—a phrase used by Paul to Timothy in 2 Timothy 2:23, thus showing another significant correlation between these two passages.

## A BASIC UNDERSTANDING OF SCRIPTURE

A man who is "able to teach" not only is self-controlled and convinced that the Word of God is true, but he also understands the Scriptures sufficiently to "be able to exhort in sound doctrine and to refute those who contradict" (Titus 1:9). We cannot communicate without knowledge! Thus Paul wrote to Timothy: "And the things which you have heard from me in the presence of many witnesses, these entrust to faithful men, who will be able to teach others also" (2 Tim. 2:2).

As maturing Christians, then, we must constantly be in the process of learning more of God's Word and understanding it. "Be diligent," said Paul, "to present yourself approved to God as a workman who is not to be ashamed, handling accurately the word of truth" (2 Tim. 2:15).

## TO SUM UP

Thus a man who is "able to teach" must be possessed with three significant qualities. First, he must be characterized by spiritual and emotional maturity, able to handle himself in threatening situations. Second, he must have a firm conviction that the Word of God is true. Third, he must understand its teachings sufficiently to be "able to teach" all men. In short, a maturing Christian must:

*Learn* more and more of the Word of God (2 Tim. 2:2).

*Believe* more and more of the Word of God (Titus 1:9).

*Live* more and more of the Word of God (2 Tim. 2:24,25).

## A PERSONAL PROJECT

The following project is designed to help you develop the quality of being "able to teach."

## Step A

Realize that every Christian man (and woman) must strive to develop this quality. It is essential for being a good father and a good mother, as well as a functioning member of the body of Christ. Parents are to teach their children (Eph. 6:4), and all members of the body of Christ are to teach and admonish one another (Col. 3:16). To be "able to teach" is a mark of Christian maturity.

## Step B

Develop a regular program of Bible study—either personally or in a group or both.

*Note:* This should be more than devotional study. It should be serious Bible study, designed to learn the basic content and doctrines of the Bible.

### SUGGESTIONS

1. Take a Bible correspondence course.

2. Enroll in a Bible class, such as one that is offered at an evening Bible institute or college.

3. Become involved in a Bible study group in your church—preferably a discussion type, where you are able to participate by asking questions and actually helping to lead the study.

## Step C

Begin to develop your personality so as to be non-threatened when discussing the Word of God and related subjects with all types of people.

*Warning:* A mere knowledge of Scripture and doctrine will not automatically solve your personality problems. Many people who know the Bible from cover to cover are defensive and highly threatened people, frequently causing them to use the Scriptures as a "personal" sword rather than the "sword of the Spirit."

**SUGGESTIONS**

1. If people attack you personally, never retaliate out of threat of embarrassment. Respond warmly and with openness. Draw them out even more.

*Note:* If you are too emotional at the moment to respond objectively, it is better to refrain from commenting until you have developed a degree of objectivity and are in control of yourself.

*Remember:* "A soft answer turns away wrath, but a harsh word stirs up anger" (Prov. 15:1).

2. Try not to embarrass people publicly—even if they attack you publicly. Seek to speak to them in a private setting. This is even true when disciplining your children.

*Note:* This may not always be possible or even advisable, but it is *usually* a good principle to follow.

3. If you continue to have problems with insecurity and feelings of threat, seek out a mature Christian friend or counselor and get help. Try to understand the reasons for your problem. Be open and honest about the situation.

4. Begin to "gently force" yourself to function in threatening situations. This is hard! But it is necessary. You will develop confidence as you begin to act and succeed in areas that are threatening.

*Warning:* Don't run away when you fail. Learn from the failure, and the next time you will succeed.

*And Remember:* The more you succeed, the more confidence you will develop.

## Step D

Once you have begun to study the Scriptures systematically and to overcome your personality problems, you are ready to start thinking creatively regarding the teaching-learning process; that is, how to use effective methods to help people learn.

**SUGGESTIONS**

1. Enroll in a class designed to help you learn *how* to teach. Better yet, begin to teach! Learn by experience. Have someone evaluate your methodology.

*Remember:* Teaching involves more than working with a group. It is also one to one (1 Thess. 2:11). In fact, this is the type of teaching that you will find the most productive.

# NOT ADDICTED TO WINE

*An overseer, then,*
*must be above reproach,*
*the husband of one wife,*
*temperate, prudent,*
*respectable, hospitable,*
*able to teach,*
**not addicted to wine** . . .
*1 Timothy 3:2,3; Titus 1:7*

If Paul were living today in our twentieth-century Western culture, would he condone drinking alcoholic beverages? Not necessarily, as will be shown later. But the issue before us in 1 Timothy and Titus is *not* total abstinence from any form of alcoholic beverage. The basic word *paroinos* used in these verses literally means a man who "sits too long at his wine." In other words, he *overdrinks,* and consequently is brought into bondage and loses control of his senses.

The Bible, therefore, does not teach total abstinence. As Unger reminds us, in most of the passages in the Old Testament where the common word for wine is used, "It certainly means fermented grape juice."[1] And the same is true in the New Testament. There is no way to prove that references to wine were to only unfermented grape juice. Rather, all cultural and exegetical evidence seems to point to the opposite conclusion.

The same is true regarding the subject before us. A mature man of God is *not* to be "addicted to wine." Paul was emphatic, both in his letter to Timothy (1 Tim. 3:3) and to Titus (Titus 1:7). He did not say he could not *partake* of wine; he said he was not to be *addicted* to it.

The Scriptures are clear! No Christian was to allow himself to be affected in a negative way by strong drink. Though they do not teach total abstinence per se, both the Old and New Testament speak in no uncertain terms regarding drunkenness. It is out of order!

Paul, in writing to the Ephesians, says: "And do not get drunk with wine, for that is dissipation, but be filled with the Spirit" (Eph. 5:18). And Peter reminds us that drunkenness is part of a life-style practiced by many non-Christians and certainly is not walking in the will of God (1 Pet. 4:2,3).

And in the book of Proverbs we read:

"Who has woe? Who has sorrow? Who has contentions? Who has complaining? Who has wounds without cause? Who has redness of eyes? Those who linger long over wine, those who go to taste mixed wine. Do not look on the wine when it is red, when it sparkles in the cup, when it goes down smoothly; at the last it bites like a serpent, and stings like a viper. Your eyes will see strange things, and your mind will utter perverse things. And you will be like one who lies down in the middle of the sea, or like one who lies down on the top of a mast" (Prov. 23:29-34).

## A HIGHER PRINCIPLE

Though Paul did not teach total abstinence and though he instructed Timothy to "use a little wine" for health reasons, he also told the Romans that "it is good not to eat meat or drink wine, or to do anything by which your brother stumbles" (Rom. 14:21).

You see, cultures vary! In New Testament days, wine was a very common drink, as it is in other cultures today. Furthermore, the degree of alcoholic content varied. In some cultures, attitudes toward drinking has connotations that are also different.

The problem Paul was referring to in Romans 14 was not the *meat* or the *wine* per se. Rather it was the idolatrous associations and the problems partaking may have created for weak Christians. There are times, Paul was saying, that total abstinence is the better way to live. *Love for others is a higher principle* and a mature, sensitive Christian is willing to avoid certain activities, even if they may be legitimate in themselves.

Thus we have two direct teachings from the Word of God regarding strong drink. First, to be addicted to it and negatively influenced by it is forbidden. It is a mark of Christian immaturity.

Second, there are times and situations when total abstinence is the best way to live. To partake may cause a weak Christian to stumble and sin against God. Every Christian must be cautious to follow this higher principle whenever it is necessary.

## A BROADER PRINCIPLE

But let's go a step further. Though Paul makes

no specific mention of other forms of indulgence in 1 Timothy 3 and Titus 1, the Bible is clear that to allow one's self to be controlled by *anything* is sin. For example, Solomon wrote:

"Listen, my son, and be wise, and direct your heart in the way. Do not be with heavy drinkers of wine, or with gluttonous eaters of meat; for the heavy drinker and the glutton will come to poverty, and drowsiness will clothe a man with rags" (Prov. 23:19-21).

You see, overeating is just as sinful as over-drinking. This is probably the great American sin— including many Christians. In fact, some Christians who would never take a drop of wine overeat with every degree of regularity. In this case, who is sinning?

A Christian is to do nothing that would harm his body or make himself an ineffective instrument for Jesus Christ (1 Cor. 6:19,20). Whether it is drink, food, tobacco, money, or just plain laziness, in no way is a Christian to allow himself to be controlled. Thus Paul says, "Whether then you eat or drink or whatever you do, do all to the glory of God" (1 Cor. 10:31).

## A PERSONAL PROJECT

The following personal project is designed to help you develop a Christian life-style that conforms to biblical principles.

### Step A

Come to grips with your own attitudes and prejudices. You may consider yourself a mature Christian, having developed certain boundaries for your own life. In doing so, have you made absolute for other Christians what God has created to be a freedom?

For example, God has allowed you the freedom to totally abstain from any alcoholic beverage. But he has given other Christians freedom to partake, though as has been shown, He has set definite boundaries.

Are you judging your brother who is taking a Christian liberty you do not take? If you are, you are violating a commandment of God. Listen to the apostle Paul: "Let not him who eats (or drinks) regard with contempt him who does not eat, and let not him who does not eat judge him who eats, for God has accepted him . . . . One man regards one day above another, another regards every day alike. Let each man be fully convinced in his own mind" (Rom. 14:3,5).

The only biblical basis any Christian has for admonishing a brother who takes this liberty is: first, he is over-indulging and hurting himself and his testimony; and second, he is causing weaker Christians to stumble and sin.

## Step B

Is there anything in *your life* that violates the broader principle? What do you do as a Christian that *harms* your body or *clouds* your thinking, or brings you into bondage to yourself?

*Remember:* A mature Christian faces his problems and solves them. The following specific suggestions may help you:

1. Isolate the problem.

2. Discuss it with several other mature Christians to see if they concur that it is really a problem or just an over-sensitive conscience.

3. If they concur that it is a real problem, ask them to pray regularly for you.

4. Develop a regular time to study the Scriptures, and to meditate and pray about the problem.

5. Write out the problem on a piece of paper, and then write out a specific goal that you wish to accomplish in overcoming the problem. Read your goal several times a day if necessary.

*Remember:* Many Christians fail consistently because they are "programmed for failure." If you want to overcome a problem, then "program yourself for victory in Jesus Christ."

6. Some have found that a period of fasting and praying has helped them break habits that are dominating and sinful.

7. If you cannot overcome your problem through personal encounter with God and through the prayers of other members of the body of Christ, then seek help from a competent Christian counselor. It may be that there are deeper roots to your problem that you need to understand and come to grips with. For example, over-drinking and over-eating are frequently a reflection of emotional problems. If this is true, you need to understand the problem and you need professional help to support you and guide you in overcoming your problem.

**Footnotes**

1. Merrill F. Unger, *Unger's Bible Dictionary*, p. 1168.

90

# 10
## NOT SELF-WILLED

*For the overseer*
*must be above reproach*
*as God's steward,*
**not self-willed** . . .
*Titus 1:7*

Have you ever met a person who always has to have his own way? Whether it is a family matter, a church matter, or a business matter? This kind of person is seldom willing to give up his own desires for the sake of the group. And when he does succumb, he does so grudgingly. "Okay," he says, "but it is not the best way to do it, or the best place to go, or the best idea." Thayer describes this characteristic as self-pleasing and arrogant. In short, a self-willed man builds the world around himself. He is self-centered and wants to "do as he pleases" (Beck). A man who is not self-willed is "not stubborn," translates Williams.

## THE ULTIMATE EXTREME
The original word translated *self-willed* in Titus 1:7 is used in only one other place in the New Testa-

ment, in 2 Peter 2:10. Here it is used in a larger context—one rich in meaning. Peter is warning Christians against false teachers and how to recognize them. They "will follow their sensuality . . . and in their greed, they will exploit you with false words" (2:2,3). They "despise authority." They will be "daring" and "self-willed" (2:10). Their hearts are "trained in greed" (2:14), and they speak out "arrogant words of vanity" (2:18).

The profile is clear. The self-willed man is a self-centered man. He is his *own authority*. And he is greedy and vain.

"But," you say, as you breathe a sigh of relief, "that certainly doesn't describe me!"

I hope not, for this is "self-centeredness" carried to the ultimate extreme. This describes the type of self-centered and self-willed behavior in Sodom and Gomorrah (2 Pet. 2:6). And it describes the stubborn conduct of a Balaam "who loved the wages of unrighteousness" (2 Pet. 2:15).

## A MORE SUBTLE FORM

But there are ways to be "self-willed"—yes, as a Christian—that are far less glaring and flagrant. But it's sinful behavior just the same, and certainly a mark of immaturity, both spiritually and psychologically.

For example, Jim has a wife and four children. Talk to them and they will tell you he is a self-willed man. Sure, he is a Christian, and he even gets his family to church every Sunday, *and* on time. And he has family devotions *at least* every other day. And he tries to be a good provider! But his wife and children will tell you he runs his home like a dictator (at least he thinks he does). He makes all the decisions. They have very little choice or say about anything. (But, of course, they have all discovered ways to circumvent him when he is gone in order to do their own thing.)

Or take Sam. He is on the church board, supposedly to be an elder. Ninety percent of the time he is the only one against an idea. He always votes "no" if the others vote "yes." And the other 10 percent of the time that he is in agreement is when *he* initiated the idea.

And then there's Jack. He works in a local factory. His nickname behind his back is "Mr. Arrogant." "He thinks he's never wrong!" say his fellow employees. "And he will never admit he has made a mistake," reports his boss, "even when everybody else knows he has." And most tragic, of course, he tries to share his faith!

## BASIC CAUSES

There are reasons for this kind o oehavior. First, some people have just *learned* to be self-centered and self-willed. They are spoiled and conceited. They were overindulged as children. They always had their own way, and they *still* want their own way even at 65!

A person who develops these personality traits *outside* of the context of Christian ethics is a candidate for sensual and selfish living that defies description. But a person who develops these traits *within* the context of Christianity often lives a life of "pious behavior" in certain realms, but turns into a very self-ish and self-centered person just the same. And frequently he rationalizes his behavior on some biblical grounds which has been ripped out of context. In a spiritual leadership role, he often becomes one who shepherds the flock of God "under compulsion," "for sordid gain," and constantly dominates and lords it over "those allotted to his charge" (1 Pet. 5:2,3).

But second, there is another basic reason why some people become extremely self-willed. It is much more difficult to understand and sometimes hard to detect even by the person himself. When talking openly about the problem, a person may blurt out, "I really don't *know why* I am so negative!" Or "I really don't understand my selfishness!"

This type of self-willed behavior is frequently related to early childhood. Between ages two and three a child goes through a natural self-will phase. It is a normal phase in every child's life, a time when he moves from extreme dependency to independence. It is biological as well as psychological. He begins to learn to control the world around him, including people.

Some people desperately misunderstand this phase of child behavior. They immediately become fearful that their child is suddenly becoming overly strong-willed. They envision a child who will grow up trying to control others the rest of his life. Rather than seeing this natural bent as one of God's greatest gifts to the child that needs to be channeled and directed, their attack is to try to "break" the child's will. Unfortunately, they only end up crushing it, causing the child to repress strong, aggressive feelings. Often these emotions are buried deep within the child, and periodically try to emerge but again are repressed.

Tragically, this unfortunate approach often produces the opposite effect of what parents had in mind. Rather than overcoming the self-willed syndrome, which automatically happens at about age three or four when the will is naturally channeled, the child instead grows into a strongly self-willed person, also, as an adult. This kind of person honestly has difficulty understanding *why* he is so self-centered and hard to get along with. But it is relatively easy to understand when you understand the psychological roots. Unfortunately it is not as easy to overcome the problem.[1]

## TO SUM UP

A strong self-will, generally speaking, can come from two sources. First, we may be overindulged, pampered and spoiled. We have been given too much freedom and too many bad examples. As a Christian or as a non-Christian, this kind of experience can produce selfishness and self-centered behavior.

Second, rather than there being *too much* freedom, we may have been overly restricted and repressed. Our natural self-will phase was never culminated, leading naturally to more cooperative traits. And to this day we are still trying to get through this phase of learning to control the world, but never achieving our goal. Deep-rooted feelings of resentment and bitterness may still be controlling us, getting us into trouble with others around us with every degree of regularity.

But whatever the source—whether spiritual or psychological—we are not mature Christians when we are self-willed. We need to face ourselves realistically and, by God's grace, overcome the problem.

## A PERSONAL PROJECT
This personal project is designed to help you overcome self-centered and self-willed behavior.

### Step A
Develop a proper perspective on self-will. A "strong will" is not necessarily the same as "self-will," as Paul uses the term. *Will power* is one of the greatest possessions you have. But a spiritually and psychologically mature Christian does not use his will power to dominate and crush others. He is also able to maintain a balance between being strong willed and humble. The apostle Paul himself was certainly this kind of man.

### Step B
If "self-will" is a problem for you, and to a certain extent it is a problem for all Christians, attempt to isolate the cause. Is it because of overindulgence, or is it because of being overly restricted?

*Clue:* A person who is self-willed because of overindulgence and the development of bad habits can usually isolate the problem rather quickly. He knows what his problem is.

On the other hand, a person who is self-willed because of being overly restricted or repressed, frequently has difficulty isolating the problem. This is because the behavior stems primarily from unconscious motivations.

## Step C

Proceed to solve your problem. If you are self-willed because you've *always* been allowed to get your own way, then *stop acting that way!* It is really that simple. Allow Jesus Christ to control you. Study the Word of God. Find out what the Bible says about being a gracious, loving and unselfish Christian and then start loving people. Stop using them for your own ends. Allow the Holy Spirit through the Word of God to produce His fruit in your life.

"But the fruit of the Spirit is love, joy, peace, patience, kindness, goodness, faithfulness, gentleness, self-control; against such things there is no law. Now those who belong to Christ Jesus have crucified the flesh with its passions and desires. If we live by the Spirit, let us also walk by the Spirit. Let us not become boastful, challenging one another, envying one another" (Gal. 5:22-26).

However, if your problem has psychological roots that are difficult to understand, you may need some professional help from a competent Christian counselor. You may need someone who can help you undertand *why* the problem exists, and then help you to set up *goals* for overcoming the problem.

*Warning:* Frequently people who have problems of this nature tend to rationalize their behavior once they understand *why* and continue to live irresponsible lives; going on in their sin, while at the same time blaming someone else for creating their problems.

*Remember:* God holds *all* men responsible for their actions, no matter what the cause of the problem. He understands and sympathizes, but we must begin to act responsibly through the resources which He gives us.

**Footnotes**

1. An overly restricted child can also develop a "weak will." He just gives up and the rest of his life he is afraid to project and exert himself.

# 11

# NOT QUICK-TEMPERED

*For the overseer*
*must be above reproach*
*as God's steward,*
*not self-willed,*
**not quick-tempered** . . .
*Titus 1·7*

A mature man of God is not prone to anger. Putting it in more contemporary fashion, "he doesn't have a short fuse."

But notice! The Bible nowhere classifies *all* anger as sin. In fact, Paul states: "Be angry, and yet do not sin . . ." (Eph. 4:26). Here Paul, of course, is not encouraging "anger"; rather he is concerned that when Christians do get angry, they should not sin in the process. Anger, like love, is a part of the very nature of God Himself. And man being made in the image of God has an unusual capacity for both.

## WHEN IS ANGER SINFUL?

Anger is sinful when it rises too soon. This is the concept inherent in Paul's statement in Titus 1:7. A

Christian is not to be "quick-tempered"; to allow himself to become *suddenly* upset and disturbed. This kind of man "flies off the handle." He is not in control of his own spirit. He is easily threatened and is quick to retaliate.

Anger is also sinful when it is prolonged. Following Paul's instruction to "be angry and yet do not sin," he added: "Do not let the sun go down on your anger, and do not give the devil an opportunity" (Eph. 4:26,27).

Sinful anger is a "brooding" kind of anger. It continues to smolder and seeks revenge. It is characterized by bitterness. It is subjective and causes a man to lose perspective. It carries a grudge, looking for an opportunity to get even. This kind of anger leads a man to "pay back evil for evil" (Rom. 12:17).

Sinful anger is also "man centered." It takes the law into its own hands. It tries to play "god." It is revengeful and impatient. It is a selfish, "personal" reaction. This kind of anger, says James, does not "achieve the righteousness of God" (Jas. 1:20).

Listen to Paul:

"Never pay back evil for evil to anyone. Respect what is right in the sight of all men. If possible, so far as it depends on you, be at peace with all men. Never take your own revenge, beloved, but leave room for the wrath of God, for it is written, 'Vengeance is mine, I will repay says the Lord. But if your enemy is hungry, feed him, and if he is thirsty, give him a drink; for in so doing you will heap burning coals upon his head.' Do not be overcome by evil, but overcome evil with good" (Rom. 12:17-21).

To sum up, then, *anger is sinful* when it arises too

soon; when it is prolonged; and when it takes the law into its own hands, attempting to pay back evil for evil. This kind of anger reflects a life-style, usually accompanied by other selfish manifestations, such as "wrath, malice, slander, and abusive speech." Christians are to "put them all aside," wrote Paul, including "anger" (Col. 3:8).

## BASIC CAUSES FOR ANGER

There are various reasons why people—both Christians and non-Christians—have a problem with anger. First, it can be *learned* through a negative example. This is what is meant in Proverbs. "Do not associate with a man given to anger; or go with a hot-tempered man, lest you learn his ways, and find a snare for yourself" (Prov. 22:24,25).

Unfortunately a child who is exposed to a parent who is quick-tempered cannot escape from the environment. He may grow up manifesting the same characteristic. The child who is constantly "yelled at" learns to yell back, if not at parents, at others. This kind of behavior easily becomes a part of his overall life-style.

A second cause for quick-tempered behavior is *selfishness*. There is the self-centered, self-willed person who has developed a life-style that includes, first of all, *himself*, and then a few people he can use for his own ends. If anyone gets in his way, he flies off the handle. Even his "friends" are victims. Let *any-one* cross him and there are "fireworks." This kind of person delights in carrying a grudge. He looks for regular opportunities to get even—particularly with anyone who "crosses him" or challenges his high and mighty position.

This type of person has become the way he is, first, because we all have the capacity to do so. Our Adamic nature is basically selfish. It wants its own way and wants to be the center of everything. But this kind of quick-tempered person is often reflecting habits of life that have developed from childhood. An overindulged, spoiled child can grow into a self-willed and quick-tempered adult. A child who throws "temper tantrums" to control people—and finds it works, can become a person who eventually throws "adult temper tantrums." He may have a more sophisticated way to do it, rather than kicking and rolling around on the supermarket floor—but he does it just the same.

For example, John is such a person. A spoiled child, he is now a spoiled adult. He used to control his parents by losing his temper in public, crying and screaming and rolling around on the floor. To avoid embarrassment his parents let him have his way. Now, thirty years later, he still does basically the same thing with his wife, his kids, and his friends, and anyone else he wants to control. At times he raises his voice, pounds the table, and uses abusive language. At other times, depending on the circumstances, he will do a "slow burn" and not speak for days. Because there is no one strong and brave enough to challenge him and then live with the aftermath of his volcanic reactions, they let him have his way.

But there is another personality type whose quick temperedness is not just a result of learning bad habits and selfishness. He is the *insecure* person; the man who becomes highly threatened. When challenged by friends or subordinates, he becomes defensive. This kind of person usually counterattacks when he feels this insecurity.

Rich is such a man. He is a professor in a Christian college. When any of his students question his procedures *or* his content, he immediately puts them down—publicly. When a fellow professor disagrees with him in faculty meetings, he immediately goes on the defensive, takes it personally, and either "blows his cool" or retreats to a more subtle way of reprisal.

There are various reasons for insecurity and defensive behavior. Most of them, however, seem to be "home grown"—the unfortunate experiences in childhood. There is the person who was always "put down" by parents, the child who never felt successful. There is the man who had a physical handicap and always felt rejected by his peers because he could not compete athletically. There is the person who grew up feeling he was ugly, with crooked teeth or unmanageable hair or a weight problem. Or he may not have been as intellectually sharp as his peers.

All of these unfortunate circumstances can lead to feelings of insecurity and inferiority. Though not every person responds to these feelings by developing a quick temper, some do. Some people actually withdraw, becoming recluses, and avoid any competition. But others develop "security" by becoming a specialist in some area of life, and then desperately react with anger when their security symbol is challenged in any way.

A fourth cause for quick-tempered tendencies relates to *parents who misunderstand the natural emotional development of a child.* Outbursts of anger appear in the typical child between his third and sixth month of life. It is the result of natural biological development, and is caused by distressful situations —hunger, gas pains, a sharp pin, an uncomfortable position, a dirty diaper, etc. It is not premeditated anger or learned, it is natural. It arises quickly, and subsides quickly if the cause for distress is eliminated. As a child grows and develops, he continues to get angry when he is unable to express himself or reach his goals and have his needs met. Again it happens quickly. A child can be very angry one minute and very happy the next.

Under normal circumstances a child learns to overcome anger tendencies and resort to more sociable ways to reach his goals. This is particularly true when he has proper behavioral models in his parents who know how to handle their own inner feelings. He learns to grow into a responsible and mature individual who does not make anger a way of life.

Parents who misunderstand the natural tendencies in small children, and who view these childhood expressions of anger through adult eyes and then overly repress the child's feelings, are going to *create* an angry adult who is "forever" trying to defend himself against those who restrict him. Be it home, church, or business, any boundaries tend to frustrate him and create bursts of anger.

Jim is such a person. In fact, his father would not even allow him to cry, even as a small child. Through fear of being punished, Jim learned to repress his feelings of distress and anger. Today he is an unhappy frustrated adult, with a chip on his shoulder. Let anyone attempt to correct him or even suggest an idea to him and he responds with anger.

But quick-temperedness, no matter what the cause, is a mark of spiritual and psychological immaturity. It must be dealt with.

## A PERSONAL PROJECT

The following project is designed to help you overcome a quick temper.

### Step A

Develop a proper biblical perspective on anger. Ask yourself the following questions and answer them "yes" or "no." Be as honest as possible.

1. Do I tend to get angry quickly?
2. Do I find that angry feelings persist and linger?
3. Do I want to take matters into my own hands and get even with others who make me angry?

If you answer "yes" to any of these questions, you are no doubt facing a sin problem in your life. Confess your sin to God and claim forgiveness through the blood of Christ (1 John 1:9).

*Note:* Be honest with God. If you have an anger problem, don't try to fake it. Tell God how you feel, confess that it is sin, and ask Him to help you overcome it.

### Step B

Proceed to isolate the cause or causes of your anger problem.

1. Is it because of a bad parental example?

2. Is it because of being spoiled and developing into a self-centered person?

3. Is it because of insecurity?

4. Is it because of an over-restricted childhood?

*Note:* Most individuals who have anger problems are victims of several of these causes. You may need to talk with someone you can trust, who can listen objectively to your problem and help you isolate the causes.

## Step C

**PROBLEM SOLUTIONS**

Take action to overcome your problem. The following suggestions will help you:

1. No matter what the cause, don't blame your problem on someone else. Don't feel you have to seek revenge. Allow God to make things right.

2. Learn to overcome your problem through an intelligent and rational approach. In days past—and even today—psychologists who worked with "angry" and "aggressive" people often encouraged them to express their anger in a non-hurtful way. However, recent research reveals that this only encourages the development of bad habits and really doesn't solve the problem. In other words, you cannot solve a childhood problem by having an adult react in childish ways. An adult must approach the problem on a rational and responsible level.

3. Set specific goals for your life in the specific areas where you are troubled. Write out these goals and read them over regularly and ask God to help you achieve them.

If you have learned to get angry through a bad example, learn to manifest Christ-like characteristics. For example, set up "patience" as a goal for the situations that really bother you.

If you are a spoiled, self-centered person, get your eyes off yourself and on others. See what you can do for others, rather than always thinking of what others can do for you.

If you are insecure and easily threatened, program yourself to avoid a negative and defensive response when someone challenges your ideas. Rather, learn to listen and ask more questions.

If you are an "angry" person because of an overly restricted childhood, learn to respond to people in positive ways. Don't allow yourself to continue to react in childish ways. Don't allow unconscious motivations to control you and cause you to strike out at others. Reprogram your reactions, and you will find that you will be instantly rewarded with positive responses from others.

**PREVENTIVE MAINTENANCE**

As mentioned earlier, every person has a natural tendency to become angry. And every person needs a program to keep their emotions under control. Following are some suggestions:

1. Stay in tune spiritually. Avoid getting out of fellowship with God. Keep your prayer life in order and listen to the voice of God as He speaks through the Scriptures.

2. Avoid having to face difficult and tense situations when you are physically and emotionally tired.

3. Engage in a regular program of physical exer-

cise, especially if you work under pressure and consistent tension.

*Note:* Housewives who are cooped up all day with children are no exception.

4. If you become angry and upset over some situation, and you are unable to shake the problem, learn to express your feelings in an objective and straightforward manner. Don't brood! Communicate.

5. Learn to back off of every aggravating situation and try to look at it objectively. Why did it happen? What problems may the other person involved be facing? Ask yourself what you can do to help become a part of the solution rather than the problem.

6. Finally, memorize James 1:19,20. If anger is a problem in your life, meditate on these verses every morning before you begin your day's activities, and then ask God to help you put this truth into practice.

"This you know, my beloved brethren. But let every one be quick to hear, slow to speak, and slow to anger; for the anger of man does not achieve the righteousness of God."

# 12
## NOT PUGNACIOUS

*For the overseer*
*must be above reproach*
*as God's steward,*
*not self-willed,*
*not quick-tempered,*
*not addicted to wine,*
**not pugnacious** . . .
*Titus 1:7*

The translators of the *New American Standard Bible* chose the word "pugnacious." It is a very appropriate word, but it may be a vague word, even to the average English-speaking person.

When you read the *King James,* there is no question as to what it means to be pugnacious. A mature man of God is not to be a "striker"—one who physically strikes out at others. Pugnaciousness then is really anger out of control, not just verbally, but physically.

Note that Paul uses this word in both his letter to Timothy and the one to Titus (1 Tim. 3:3; Titus 1:7), and in both instances it follows the phrase, "not addicted to wine." The connection, of course, is clear! A person who loses control of his senses because of "too much wine" also tends to lose control of his anger. Many a brawl has come out of a barroom scene, where people have had too much to drink.

Why would Paul have to refer to such an obvious characteristic? Wouldn't any thinking person know that physical violence is out of character with Christian behavior? The same question can be asked about being a "husband of one wife." Isn't it obvious that living with more than one woman is a violation of God's plan for marriage?

These questions are not difficult to answer when we stop and think about the pagan culture and lifestyle out of which these New Testament Christians were converted. Writing to the Corinthians, Paul said, "Do not be deceived; neither fornicators, nor idolators, nor adulterers, nor effeminate, nor homosexuals, nor thieves, nor covetous, nor drunkards, nor revilers, nor swindlers, shall inherit the Kingdom of God." Then Paul adds: "And such were some of you" (1 Cor. 6:9-11). New Testament leaders had to constantly warn against allowing characteristics from a previous pagan life-style to continue on in the Christian life. Paul admonished the Ephesians and the Colossians to "put away" these things and to walk worthy of their calling in Christ (Eph. 4:17-32; Col. 3:1-14).

And so, a spiritual leader is to be mature in controlling his human spirit. Not only is he to be a person who is not "quick tempered," but he is not to engage in physical violence.

## SOME BIBLICAL EXAMPLES

The Scriptures give us several unique illustrations

of what happens when a man loses control in this area of his life. God's displeasure is obvious, even when it happens to His choicest servants.

### CAIN

Perhaps the most tragic story occurred early in human history. Cain became jealous because God favored his brother's offering. Rather than conforming to the will of God, his anger and hatred toward Abel —*and* God—culminated in murder. As a result, God punished Cain severely. Though God spared his life, Cain was plagued the rest of his days with a curse for his evil deeds (Gen. 4:1-15).

### MOSES

Moses, of course, was one of God's choicest servants. But he got into serious trouble when he lost his temper and slew an Egyptian. Though God overruled in this situation, it appears that Moses was trying to take matters into his own hands. He was not sensitive to the Lord's timing, and he was ready to become the "deliverer" on his own, and ahead of God's schedule (Acts 7:20-29).

Evidently Moses never completely overcame his tendency to "strike out" when he became angry. After he had received the Ten Commandments from God on the mountain and when he saw the people engaged in idolatry, in a fit of anger he threw the tablets of stone on the ground and shattered them to pieces (Exod. 32:19).

God's sympathy was with Moses. He replaced the tablets (Exod. 34:1). But on another occasion shortly before God was to lead the children of Israel into the Promised Land, Moses disobeyed God by striking a rock twice to bring forth water, rather than speaking to the rock as God had commanded. Consequently God disciplined Moses, His choice servant, in not allowing him to enter the Promised Land (Num. 20:1-13).

Again Moses had allowed his anger to express itself out of the will of God. And again he took matters into his own hands. He actually spoke as if the flow of water depended on himself (20:10). And this time—for all to see—God punished Moses. Moses had conveyed the wrong signals to the people, and God did not allow this to go uncorrected, even though it meant disciplining the man He had allowed to come into His very presence.

## PETER

And then there was Peter! An aggressive and impetuous man, he too took matters into his own hands. He had bragged about his courage never to forsake the Lord! And to save face, when the soldiers had come to take Jesus, he drew his sword and struck out at Malchus missing his neck and severing his ear from his head. Jesus admonished Peter to put away his sword. Publicly embarrassed, Peter became angry and ran off into the night and later denied the Lord three times (John 18:1-27).

There is plenty of biblical evidence to demonstrate that God is displeased with physical violence. True, at certain times God actually used the children of Israel themselves to judge unrighteous nations. But God disapproves of uncontrollable anger that is motivated by personal vindictiveness. In fact, Jesus Christ set the highest standard for personal relationships known to man when He said: "You have heard that it was said, 'an eye for an eye and a tooth for a tooth.' But I say unto you, do not resist him who is evil; but whoever slaps you on your right cheek, turn to him the other also" (Matt. 5:38,39).

## SOME TWENTIETH CENTURY APPLICATIONS

It is interesting how cultural demands change human behavior. And perhaps a culture touched by Christianity is the most significant example.

Take our twentieth-century culture! Historically, physical violence against other human beings has been generally condemned, both in the laws of our land and in the minds and hearts of people. Our social conscience has been repulsed by child abuse, wife beating, and antisocial behavior against people generally. Even police brutality against criminals has become an issue.

Unfortunately the general change in moral values that has affected our culture in the last decade or two is also changing our attitudes towards violence. The day will no doubt come when our social conscience that has been historically tuned to the Protestant ethic will be so perverted we will suffer little emotional pain over physical violence against other human beings. But it is still true, thank God, that as a people we are generally conscience-stricken by pugnacious behavior.

But underneath and down deep, man has not changed. He may be culturally conditioned against certain attitudes and actions, but when put under pressure and personally threatened, he can develop

118

other ways of "striking out." In fact, verbal abuse in our culture can be even more effective in hurting others. It is much easier to recover from physical bruises and even broken bones than to recover from a bad reputation and a broken heart. Unfortunately some Christians develop the art of verbal attack. And what makes it so tragic is that such behavior is actually disguised as personal concern. It sounds spiritual to share morsels of gossip in the context of prayer—to say, for example, "Don't tell anybody but. . . ."

"The heart," said Jeremiah, "is more deceitful than all else and is desperately sick; who can understand it?" (Jer. 17:9). Yes, even the Christian's heart! Gossip and malicious talk, especially when disguised as spiritual concern, is the most dangerous form of twentieth-century "pugnaciousness."

But there is another application we need to look at. It is child discipline. True, the Bible speaks of discipline. But it is always to be administered in love. It is never to be used as an escape valve for displaced hostility. How easy it is to rationalize behavior, to swing a rod when emotional and out of control, and then to tell ourselves we are doing it for the sake of the child!

A mature man of God, then, is "no striker"—either verbally or physically. He is in control of his human spirit, even on the rare occasions when he is angry with proper motives.

## A PERSONAL PROJECT

The project designed for overcoming a "quick temper" is also applicable to overcoming pugnacious behavior. However, here are some additional suggestions for dealing with this problem.

## Step A

Be sure you have not developed subtle ways to hurt people, other than through physical attack. Ask yourself the following questions:

1. How frequently do I talk about other people's problems?

2. With whom do I share this information?

3. How often do I repeat information about a *particular* person?

4. What kind of emotional reaction do I have when I talk about somebody else's problems?

If you talk frequently about others and to a variety of people, and if you tend to repeat stories about a particular person and if you enjoy doing so, chances are you are "getting even" with someone. You are using a more culturally acceptable form of pugnacious behavior, but it is "striking out" just the same.

## Step B

Make sure you are following a biblical approach to handling personal offense and forgiveness. Study carefully Matthew 5:21-24; 18:15-17,21,22.

## Step C

Once you have isolated areas of resentment in your own personality, proceed to deal with them. You might follow this sequence:

1. Confess your sin to God.

2. Pray for God's help in overcoming the problem.

3. Write out some specific goals to help you overcome your problem. For example, you might write "I will not talk about (Jim or Jane, etc.) in a derogatory way."

Or "I will talk personally to (Jim or Jane) about their problem. If they have hurt me, I will communicate with them face to face rather than get even through gossiping about them."

4. If you have hurt someone's reputation, ask them to forgive you.

## Step D

If you have a serious and persistent problem with anger and loss of emotional and physical control, and if you have not been able to overcome the problem through the previous suggestions, then seek professional help from a Christian psychiatrist or psychologist. You may need someone to help you analyze the problem and support you in overcoming it.

*Warning:* Don't expect someone else to solve your problem. They can only assist you. *You* must take the initiative and become a mature person in Jesus Christ—no matter how difficult it is.

# 13
## UNCONTENTIOUS

*An overseer, then,*
*must be above reproach,*
*the husband of one wife,*
*temperate, prudent, respectable,*
*hospitable, able to teach,*
*not addicted to wine or*
*pugnacious, but gentle,*
**uncontentious** *. . .*
*1 Timothy 3:2,3*

Tom is a smart, outgoing successful businessman. He is president of his own company . . . and is doing well—in fact, very well!

He enjoys being "top dog." His relatively small staff works hard to carry out his orders.

Six months ago Tom was elected to serve as an elder in his church, but there was something about Tom that no one really knew. As long as he was "calling the shots" and "making all the decisions," he was happy, easy to live with, and cooperative. But when he was just one among equals, it was a different story.

To everyone's surprise, Tom always seemed to take an opposite point of view from everyone else on the board. If it was his idea, fine! But if the ideas came from someone else, he could never seem to get excited about it. In fact, he would do all he could to find reasons *why* it wasn't workable. Needless to say,

Tom literally destroyed the unity among this group of men. His *contentious* attitude and behavior became an almost invincible roadblock to consensus. He forced a vote on every issue, which usually came out 8 to 1 against Tom.

## CONTENTIOUSNESS—WHAT IS IT?

The Greek word for contentious (*amachos*) is used only twice in the New Testament, in the list of qualifications for an elder in 1 Timothy 3 and in Titus 3:2. The context in which it is used in 1 Timothy 3, of course, is very significant. A spiritual leader is not to be "addicted to wine or pugnacious, but gentle, uncontentious. . . ." Beck translates: ". . . no drunkard, not violent, but gentle, not quarrelsome. . . ."

There is a similar context in Titus 3:2. Here, however, Paul is speaking to Christians generally. He exhorts Titus to remind them "to be subject to rulers, to authorities, to be obedient, to be ready for every good deed, to malign no one, to be uncontentious. . . ." Williams translates: "Constantly remind people to submit to and obey the rulers who have authority over them, so as to be ready for any good enterprise, to stop abusing anyone, to be peaceable. . . . Interestingly, Paul includes the *total* scope of humanity—rulers, authorities, *all* men. And he excludes no Christian. "These things speak and exhort and reprove with all authority," wrote Paul. "Let no one disregard you" (Titus 2:15).

A contentious person *struggled against* others, *competed* and *debated*. This was Tom's problem! He could not stand competition. He was always *one* against everyone else. He was unwilling to bend. It was either *his* way or no way! In his business he got away with it. In fact, the problem wasn't even obvious—to outsiders. He was the one and only authority, and everyone else kowtowed to his demands. After all he paid their salaries, and they knew instinctively they could be replaced. In fact, the people who chose to work for him rather enjoyed their subservient positions. After all, under these conditions, *he* was responsible—not them.

But, a biblical view of leadership in the church knows nothing of this kind of philosophy. He that is "greatest" is to be also "servant" (Matt. 23:11). There is to be no authoritarian figure running the whole show. Leaders, yes—but as a team. Someone who may put in more time and effort, and even be financially remunerated—yes (1 Tim. 5:17,18), but one among equals.

Tom was *contentious!* He certainly was not a mature Christian and obviously not qualified to be a spiritual leader in the church or his home. Even as a very successful businessman, in terms of making money, he was a total failure where it really counts.

## A POSITIVE POINT OF VIEW

When it comes to the functioning body of Christ, no concept is more important in the Scriptures than *unity*. And no concern is more upon the heart of Jesus Christ Himself! Knowing that the time was quickly coming for Him to complete the work He had come to do on earth, He prayed in earnest to the Father for His disciples—and for us:

"I do not ask in behalf of these alone, but for these also who believe in Me through their word; that they may all be one; . . . I in them, and Thou in Me, that they may be perfected in unity, that the world may know that Thou didst send Me, and didst love them, even as Thou didst love Me" (John 17:20,21,23).

Unity in the body of Christ demonstrates to the world the deity of Jesus Christ and the unity He has with God the Father. It communicates the very essence of Christianity "that God was in Christ reconciling the world to Himself" (2 Cor. 5:19).

God is particularly pleased with those individuals who strive to create unity. "Blessed are the peacemakers," said Jesus, "for they shall be called sons of God" (Matt. 5:9).

No single concept probably occupied the thinking of the apostle Paul more than the concept of *unity* and *oneness*. Listen to his words to the Roman Christians:

"Be of the same mind toward one another; do not be haughty in mind, but associate with the lowly. Do not be wise in your own estimation" (Rom. 12:16).

"If possible, so far as it depends on you, be at peace with all men" (Rom. 12:18).

"So then let us pursue the things which make for peace and the building up of one another" (Rom. 14:19).

"Now may the God who gives perseverance and encouragement grant you to be of the same mind with one another according to Christ Jesus; that with one accord you may with one voice glorify the God and Father of our Lord Jesus Christ" (Rom. 15:5,6).

And notice Paul's primary concern as he begins the practical section of his letter to the Ephesian Christians:

"I, therefore, the prisoner of the Lord, entreat you to walk in a manner worthy of the calling with which you have been called, with all humility and gentleness, with patience, showing forbearance to one another in love, being diligent to pursue the unity of the spirit in the bond of peace" (Eph. 4:1-3).

And to Timothy Paul wrote:

"But refuse foolish and ignorant speculations, knowing that they produce quarrels. And the Lord's bond-servant must not be quarrelsome, but kind to all, able to teach, patient when wronged, with gentleness correcting those who are in opposition . . ." (2 Tim. 2:23-25).

## WHAT CAUSES CONTENTIOUSNESS?

Contentious people—people who are always starting arguments and quarrels and fights—are frequently selfish and jealous people. They are motivated by "earthly wisdom."

James speaks pointedly to this issue: "But if you have bitter jealousy and selfish ambition in your heart, do not be arrogant and so lie against the truth. This wisdom is not that which comes down from above, but is earthly, natural, demonic. For where jealousy and selfish ambition exist, there is disorder and every evil thing" (Jas. 3:14-16). In contrast, James also described the results of "heavenly wisdom": "But the wisdom from above is first pure, then peaceable, gentle, reasonable, full of mercy and good fruits, unwavering, without hypocrisy" (James 3:17).

Contentious people are also often insecure people. Insecurity drives individuals in two directions. Some become reclusive and withdrawn. They seldom open their mouths and retreat from any kind of competition.

*Or,* they become domineering and authoritarian personalities. They cover up their insecurity by controlling everyone else. They can't accept defeat; it threatens them terribly, so they become "winners." They overachieve and then work like crazy to stay on top. When their position is threatened in any way, they will resort to even non-Christian tactics to defend themselves against their fear of failure.

This kind of man often puts other people down, to build himself up. He becomes a victim of a subtle, even unconscious selfishness that is reflected in all kinds of ways—authoritarianism, arguments, quarreling, gossip, backbiting, critical remarks, cursing, and even physical violence.

Christian leaders who have this problem are particularly dangerous. They tend to rationalize their behavior and even use the Word of God as a weapon to reach their self-centered goals. They interpret Scripture through their own psychological grid. They take advantage of their "spiritual" position and begin to lord it over others (1 Pet. 5:3). If anyone resists their authoritarian tactics, they quickly "beat them down" and control their opposition's conscience with such verses as, "Obey your leaders and submit to them" (Heb. 13:17).

And then there is the *bitter* person—a person who

has "let the sun go down on his anger." He has given "the devil an opportunity" in his life (Eph. 4:26,27) and this bitter spirit, which may have begun with one or two people, has generalized to include most everyone, including himself. It is reflected in a general "contentiousness"—a "chip on the shoulder" attitude that affects many people.

The writer of Hebrews spoke to this problem:

"Pursue after peace with all men, and after the sanctification without which no one will see the Lord. See to it that no root of bitterness springing up causes trouble, and by it many be defiled" (Heb. 12:14,15).

## A PERSONAL PROJECT

The following personal project is designed to help you overcome contentiousness in your personality.

### Step A

Attempt to isolate the cause or causes of your problem. Ask yourself the following questions and read each story that accompanies each question. The stories are designed to help you identify your problem.

1. Am I contentious because of *selfishness* and *jealous* attitudes?

Paul was an only child. He always got his way in everything he wanted. He early in life resented any competition. As long as he can remember he has manipulated and used other people to achieve his own ends.

2. Am I contentious because of *insecurity?*

Jim was one of several children; he had an older brother and two younger sisters. He was a normal child, of average intelligence, likeable, mildly athletic. But his brother was a genius in most every way, and he took after his father. And Jim's dad always favored the older brother, and tended to "put Jim down." Jim was *forced* to compete in every way. If he withdrew, he was teased and made fun of.

As he grew older, he learned that through real hard work and drive, he could win at most everything. His older brother's natural ability to achieve soon took on a "lazy tone" and soon Jim was outdistancing him in most everything. At last he had the "applause" of his father and others.

Unfortunately this approach to life has become a "habit pattern" for Jim. In fact, he cannot feel "security" unless he always *wins* and is the center of everything. He *must* win every argument, *must* have the final word, *must* have *his* ideas accepted.

**3. Am I contentious because of a *root of bitterness?***

John's father was an alcoholic. As long as he can remember, his dad mistreated his mother and abused the other children. As long as he can remember, he has had angry, bitter feelings toward his father. In fact, John feels anger toward most everyone now. Consequently, he is always hurting someone's feelings with nasty remarks and "put down" attitudes and statements.

## Step B

Once you feel you understand the cause of your problem, start the process of change. Start with confession, first to God and then to those you have hurt. If you have hurt the local body of Christ in which you fellowship, confess your sin to the body as a whole, and ask for their forgiveness and prayers so that you might change your attitudes and behavior.

*Note:* Public confession should be made *only* if it has affected the whole body. Seek advice from the spiritual leaders in your church as to whether or not public confession is necessary.

## Step C

Write out *specific* goals which relate to your *specific* problem with *specific* people. Read these goals every day. Use them as personal prayer requests.

If you are a contentious element in your family, you may want to write out something like this: "I will not start any quarrels when we are eating together. I will listen to what others are saying without automatically disagreeing with someone."

## Step D

If your problem persists or if you have difficulty isolating the root cause of your problem, seek out a Christian psychologist and take some psychological tests to help you understand your personality conflicts.

14
GENTLE

*An overseer, then, must be*
*above reproach, the husband*
*of one wife, temperate, prudent,*
*respectable, hospitable,*
*able to teach, not addicted to wine*
*or pugnacious, but* **gentle** *. . .*
*1 Timothy 3:2,3*

"Blessed are the gentle, for they shall inherit the earth" (Matt. 5:5). These are the words of Jesus Christ Himself as He taught the multitudes.

A gentle person reflects attitudes that are actually the opposite of several of the negative qualities we have just looked at. Paul is telling us that, by contrast, a *gentle* Christian is not quick tempered, not pugnacious, nor contentious. Rather he is a mild-mannered person characterized by meekness, forbearance, and kindness.

The translators of the *New American Standard Bible* used the word "gentle" or "gentleness" to represent several Greek words, all with basically the same meaning. And they are used in the Scriptures to describe what our attitude and behavior should be in various circumstances and situations and with various types of people.

## GENTLENESS TOWARD WHOM?

1. We must be gentle with non-Christians.

Both in his letter to Titus and Timothy, Paul instructs Christians to demonstrate an attitude of gentleness, not only toward other believers, but toward unbelievers. Writing to Titus, he said that we are to be "gentle, showing every consideration for all men" (Titus 3:2) and then Paul says "why"! Remember, he says, that "we also once were foolish ourselves, disobedient, deceived, enslaved to various lusts and pleasures, spending our life in malice and envy, hateful, hating one another" (Titus 3:3).

Paul then reminds these New Testament Christians that it was the "kindness of God our Savior and His love for mankind" that saved them and not because of their righteous deeds, but "according to his mercy" in Christ Jesus (Titus 3:4,5). In other words, says Paul, demonstrate the same gentleness and mercy toward non-Christians that God showered on you when He saved you. Be as patient with their shortcomings as the Lord was with yours.

Writing also to Timothy, Paul said that Christians are to be "patient when wronged, with gentleness correcting those who are in opposition; if perhaps God may grant them repentance leading to the knowledge of the truth . . ." (2 Tim. 2:24,25).

Paul illustrates this characteristic in his own life—and that of Silas and Timothy—when he wrote to the Thessalonians and said: "But we proved to be gentle among you, as a nursing mother tenderly cares for her children." Here in this pagan community, these New Testament leaders preached the gospel with "tender loving care."

There is no more intimate and beautiful picture of "gentleness" than that of a mother nursing her child. And Paul is not ashamed to be identified with this illustration. In Christianity, you see, there is no contradiction between being a *man's man* and being a *gentle man*.

Peter also had something to say particularly to Christian women, about a gentle spirit toward non-Christians. If you are married to a non-Christian man, he said, then win him to Christ "with the imperishable quality of a gentle and quiet spirit" (1 Pet. 3:4). There is no doubt that this quality of life —this mark of spiritual maturity—will help us communicate more effectively to those outside of Christ. Be patient! Be kind! Be gentle! Demonstrate the reality of Jesus Christ, who said, "Take My yoke upon you, and learn from Me, for I am gentle and humble of heart; and you shall find rest for your souls" (Matt. 11:29).

2. We must be gentle with carnal Christians.

"Brethren, even if a man is caught in any trespass, you who are spiritual, restore such a one in a spirit of gentleness; looking to yourself, lest you too be tempted" (Gal. 6:1).

This is to be the attitude of mature Christians toward a fellow Christian who has failed in his Christian life! No attitude of superiority! No spirit of resentment! No pride! Rather, said Paul, "Bear one another's burdens, and thus fulfill the law of Christ.

136

For if anyone thinks he is something when he is nothing, he deceives himself" (Gal. 6:2,3). Paul himself demonstrated this attitude again and again as he dealt with "sinning" Christians. Not that he was weak and non-directive. Read 1 Corinthians and Galatians. Paul spoke with authority and dealt with the nitty-gritty of the Christian life in a straightforward manner. He pulled no punches!

But as you read the writings of Paul, there is no doubt that his attitude was always one of deep concern. He disciplined in love! As he wrote to the Corinthians he said, "Now I Paul urge you by the meekness and gentleness of Christ" (2 Cor. 10:1).

3. We must be gentle with all Christians.

*All Christians* are to relate to *all other Christians* "with all humility and gentleness, with patience, showing forbearance to one another in love" (Eph. 4:2). These are the words of Paul to the Ephesians. This is the way, he said, "to preserve the unity of the Spirit in the bond of peace" (Eph. 4:3).

Writing to the Colossians, he also said: "Put on a heart of compassion, kindness, humility, gentleness, and patience; bearing with one another, and forgiving each other, whoever has a complaint against any one; just as the Lord forgave you, so also should you" (Col. 3:12,13).

"As the Lord forgave you!" Again Paul builds his argument for *gentleness* and *patience* and *kindness* on the Lord's attitude towards us. How can we, who have experienced the marvelous grace and forgiveness of God, fail to forgive those who trespass against us? All believers need to read again Jesus' story of the unjust slave who, though forgiven by his master, failed to forgive his fellow slave. (See Matt. 18:21-35.)

## A PERSONAL PROJECT
The following project is designed to help you develop the quality of gentleness in all of your relationships.

### Step A
Realize that a gentle spirit must be pursued. Listen to Paul's words to Timothy: "But flee from these things, you man of God; and pursue after righteousness, godliness, faith, love, perseverance *and* gentleness" (1 Tim. 6:11).

*Gentleness,* then, must be a goal for every Christian just as any other spiritual quality. Fortunately for some people, it comes easier. Unfortunately for others, it comes harder.

### Step B
Realize that *gentleness* is a quality that God wants to produce in your life through the Holy Spirit and His Word. "But the fruit of the Spirit is love, joy, peace, patience, kindness, goodness, faithfulness, gentleness, self-control" (Gal. 5:22,23).

But to experience the "fruit of the Spirit," we must "walk by the Spirit" (Gal. 5:25); that is, we must consciously and deliberately "put off" or abandon the deeds of the flesh and walk in the way God has outlined in His Word. God will not force us to "walk by the Spirit." *Gentleness* and all the other qualities outlined in Galatians 5:22,23 are not automatic.

They must be developed through the process of becoming more and more like Jesus Christ. And the agent that the Holy Spirit uses to create these qualities in our lives is the Word of God.

## Step C

Realize that God is ready to give wisdom to His children to enable them to "walk by the Spirit." James calls this wisdom "from above" and tells us that it is "first pure, then peaceable, gentle, reasonable, full of mercy and good fruits, unwavering, without hypocrisy" (Jas. 3:17).

Furthermore, James tells us this wisdom is available to all those who ask in faith. "But if any of you lacks wisdom, let him ask of God, who gives to all men generously and without reproach, and it will be given to him. But let him ask in faith without doubting, for the one who doubts is like the surf of the sea driven and tossed by the wind. For let not that man expect that he will receive anything from the Lord, being a double-minded man, unstable in all his ways" (Jas. 1:5-8).

## Step D

Discover those relationships in life where you have the most difficulty demonstrating "gentleness." Set up goals in these areas and then ask God to give you wisdom to become the person you should be in these relationships.

The following suggestions will help you isolate your problem areas:

1. If you are married, ask your wife and children to help make you aware of times when you are not

gentle. Sometimes we do not really know how "we sound" to others.

2. Ask a close friend to frankly evaluate your relationships with other people, to give you feedback in any area that violates a spirit of gentleness.

3. If you are a teacher, a boss, or anyone who works with people, ask them to fill out an evaluation form. Include a question regarding how they view your attitudes and behavior. Ask them to evaluate the spirit in which you do things, such as the way you give orders, make assignments, answer questions, etc.

4. Develop a regular Bible study program. There is no substitute for the Scriptures in serving as a mirror to reflect those areas in our lives which are not reflective of Jesus Christ.

# 15

## FREE FROM THE LOVE OF MONEY

*An overseer, then,*
*must be above reproach,*
*the husband of one wife, temperate,*
*prudent, respectable, hospitable,*
*able to teach, not addicted*
*to wine or pugnacious,*
*but gentle, uncontentious,*
***free from the love of money* . . .**
*1 Timothy 3:2,3*

I had the privilege of sharing in a camp ministry for a week with a doctor who serves as a medical missionary in Africa. He spoke in the morning and I in the evening. During the course of the week he related a tragic story. He told about the man who had been used by God to challenge him to become a medical missionary. This man was also a Christian doctor. He, too, had planned to go to the same hospital in Africa. But he changed his mind and decided to stay in the United States. He became a very successful doctor, building a large and prosperous practice. From the world's point of view he had everything he wanted. But something went wrong! After three unsuccessful marriages, and while still a young man, he committed suicide.

By contrast, the doctor who gave up fame and fortune (humanly speaking) continues to treat hundreds of African patients every week, and sees many of them come to know Jesus Christ as personal Saviour. In fact, while on furlough he shared the challenge of world missions with a group of teen-agers, giving up a $200-a-day salary in an American hospital to participate in this week of camp.

This story, of course, does not put a premium on poverty! Nor is it meant to "put down" Christian doctors who don't become missionaries. But it does illustrate graphically that to love money and the things money buys does not in itself make a man happy. In fact, it can lead to a bitter end.

Paul speaks of this matter in the first letter to Timothy: "But those who want to get rich fall into temptation and a snare and many foolish and harmful desires which plunge men into ruin and destruction. For the love of money is the root of all sorts of evil, and some by longing for it have wandered away from the faith, and pierced themselves with many a pang" (1 Tim. 6:9-10).

## MONEY IS NOT EVIL

It must be made clear that money in itself is not evil. The Bible does not say a Christian should be "free from money" but rather, "free from the love of money." It is a matter of priorities, Jesus said, "But seek first His kingdom, and His righteousness, and all these things [food and clothes] shall be added to you" (Matt. 6:33). A man who "loves money" lays up "treasures upon earth" rather than "treasures in heaven" (Matt. 6:19,20). And as Jesus says, "Where your treasure is, there will your heart be also" (Matt. 6:21).

The Bible then is talking about a "life-style" of a person who is more "earthly minded" than "heavenly minded." This present life, its worldly possessions, activities and benefits are more important than eternal life. There is constant seeking after more and more. Selfishness and pride take over. Thus the Scripture warns: "Let your way of life be free from the love of money, being content with what you have; for He Himself has said, 'I will never desert you, nor will I ever forsake you' " (Heb. 13:5).

## A HUMAN TENDENCY

The problem of "forgetting God" when earthly possessions multiply is not a new problem. The children of Israel faced this temptation when they entered the Promised Land. And Moses warned them ahead of time that this temptation would come. "Then it shall come about when the Lord your God brings you into the land . . . to give you, great and splendid cities which you did not build, and houses full of all good things which you did not fill, and hewn cisterns which you did not dig, vineyards and olive trees which you did not plant, and you shall eat and be satisfied, then watch yourself, lest you forget the Lord who brought you from the land of Egypt, out of the house of slavery" (Deut. 6:10-12).

And again Moses warned: "Beware lest you forget the Lord your God by not keeping His commandments. . . . Otherwise, you may say in your heart,

'My power and the strength of my hand made me this wealth' " (Deut. 8:11,17).

The most tragic epitaph in the Old Testament was recorded in the book of Judges after the children of Israel had entered the land. In spite of the warnings given by Moses, and after Joshua had passed off the scene, we read these almost unbelievable words: "And there arose another generation after them who did not know the Lord, nor yet the work which He had done for Israel. . . . So they forsook the Lord and served Baal and the Astartes" (Judg. 2:10,13).

And so, too, Christians need to learn a basic lesson from Israel. God's blessings upon us materially *can* become a curse. We can forget the One who gave it to us. It is a human tendency, and verified throughout human history. We can become so wrapped up in the material side of life that we lose spiritual perspective. Money can become an end in itself rather than a "means to godly ends."

A mature Christian has maintained a proper balance. He is "free from the love of money."

## A STATUS SYMBOL

Not only is materialism a natural human tendency, but it is also a status symbol in most cultures. A person may start out in life with relatively little. But as he accumulates a certain amount of wealth, he soon discovers he can do more with it than buy food and clothes. He learns that "money talks." It attracts friends, gives a man power, status, and security.

Obviously all of us need money to exist. It is a cultural necessity. A certain amount is necessary for security. But when we make money for selfish purposes and self-glorification, we are building on a shaky foundation. And "friends" who are "friends" because of our money are not "friends" at all.

## A DEEP PSYCHOLOGICAL NEED

Strange as it may seem—and yet not so strange—some Christians have a problem with an inordinate desire for money and material things because they have been deprived as children. They have not been able to have "those things" or "do those things" that everyone else around them has or does.

This, of course, is a culturally related problem. Man's needs are basically simple. But culture has complicated what we *feel* we need, and this is naturally true of children, though it is also true of adults. We cannot ignore these feelings. They are real. To feel "deprived" is an actuality, not a figment of the imagination.

It takes wisdom to strike a balance in a materialistic culture. To give children too much creates problems, but to withhold what is "normal" also creates problems. And it really backfires if we try to teach a child to become non-materialistic by withholding material things that are continually at the disposal of most of his peers. It may only serve to create an unsatisfied and deepening thirst *for* material things.

This phenomenon is true even in little things. For instance, take chewing gum! Some parents decide they will not let their children chew gum. They classify it as a bad habit and set up certain punishment for the children if they even ask for gum. They never keep gum in the house nor do they let them buy it.

What happens in this situation? The children, of course, learn not to ask for chewing gum at home. But they may develop an insatiable desire to chew gum, especially since their friends do and they see a lot of advertisements on television. In fact, it can become an obsession with them. In the case I am thinking of, everytime the children got away from their parents, they begged other people for chewing gum, but always learning to get rid of it before they got home, lest they be punished.

The same psychological phenomenon takes place in areas that some Christians classify as questionable activities for Christians. By making such a big deal, for example, about never going to certain places or doing certain things, they only create an unnatural desire to "sneak out and go." The same thing will happen when a child is overly deprived of material things. He may end up being materialistic—if not in fact, in heart.

## LAZY CHRISTIANS

The Bible is a marvelous book of balances. Thus, the Scriptures also have something to say about the "lazy" Christian: the one who takes advantage of others. Thus, Paul wrote: "If anyone will not work, neither let him eat. For we hear that some among you are leading an undisciplined life, doing no work at all, but acting like busybodies. Now such persons we command and exhort in the Lord Jesus Christ to work in quiet fashion and eat their own bread" (2 Thess. 3:10-12).

Some people take pride in their poverty. They justify their laziness on the basis of "not loving money." Obviously this is not what the Lord had in mind. Man is, by command from God, to earn his living by the "sweat of his brow." (See Gen. 3:17-19.)

## A PARTICULAR TEMPTATION FOR THE SPIRITUAL LEADER

The Bible is clear that spiritual leaders will be faced with particular temptations regarding money. This is why Paul, in specifying the qualifications for the elders in Crete, said they must be men who are "not fond of sordid gain" (Titus 1:7). And Peter also said to the elders in various churches: "Shepherd the flock of God among you, not under compulsion, but voluntarily, according to the will of God, and not for sordid gain, but with eagerness" (1 Pet. 5:2). The New Testament world was filled with men who had false motives. Paul called them, "rebellious men, empty talkers and deceivers," men who were "teaching things they should not teach, for the sake of sordid gain" (Titus 1:10, 11).

It must be made clear, however, that it is God's will for spiritual leaders to be cared for financially. Thus he wrote to Timothy and said: "Let the elders who rule well be considered worthy of double honor, especially those who work hard at their preaching and teaching" (1 Tim. 5:17). Paul is obviously speaking here of material remuneration. And to the Corinthians he also made it clear that those who proclaim the gospel are "to get their living from the gospel" (1 Cor. 9:14).

Some have falsely interpreted Paul's refusal on occasions to take money to mean Christians should always "make tents" and support themselves. To do so is to miss completely Paul's motive, and his total approach to financial support. At times he refused, but on other occasions he accepted gifts freely. (See Phil. 4:15,16.) When he refused, it was usually to make sure pagans did not misinterpret his motives. He was very cautious that he not be associated with false teachers who were taking advantage of people financially. Furthermore he was very concerned that people know the gospel was free. And he oftentimes "bent over backwards" to be a good example (2 Thess. 3:7-9).

Overall the lesson is clear! Spiritual leaders must be cautious. Unfortunately the twentieth-century world is also filled with religious hustlers. Even among evangelical Christians there are leaders who take advantage of Christians financially. They resort to "guilt tactics," "white lies," and "don't you feel sorry for me" innuendos to get money. When this happens it is tragic. They completely disqualify themselves in God's sight from being a mature man of God, for they are "fond of sordid gain."

But a word also needs to be said on the other side. Many American Christians particularly are notorious for taking advantage of Christian leaders who serve in various capacities and make their living as a result of a full-time ministry. They somehow feel that a pastor or missionary shouldn't be paid as much as the average man is making. Some even go so far as to think a Christian leader should serve without remuneration. Numerous Christian leaders have experienced the time when the remuneration they received for Christian ministry barely paid their travel expense.

This, of course, is just as wrong and sinful as a spiritual leader who is "fond of sordid gain." Both practices are a violation of the Word of God. Though Paul told the Ephesian elders that he had "coveted no one's silver or gold or clothes" (Acts 20:33), he also said on several occasions, "The laborer is worthy of his wages" (1 Tim. 5:18; 1 Cor. 9:9-11).

## A PERSONAL PROJECT

The following project is designed to help you evaluate your motives regarding money and material things.

### Step A

Sit down and make a list of those things that are most important to you in your life. Be honest. Write down those things that first appear in your mind.

*Warning:* You may find there are other things that surface that are just as wrong as the *love of money.*

### Step B

Refocus your priorities in the light of biblical values. Where is your heart? What motivates you the most? What are you doing with your money? Can you justify your expenditures in the light of eternal values? How much are you giving away for worthy causes?

Read carefully the following passages of Scripture to help you rearrange your priorities: Mat-

thew 6:19-34; 1 Timothy 6:6-10; Proverbs 15:27;
Proverbs 23:4,5; Proverbs 30:7-9; Ecclesiastes 5:10;
2 Corinthians 8-9.

## Step C

In the light of this study and personal evaluation,
set up *specific* goals for your life relative to "money
matters." No one can tell you what to do specifically
—except God. But these biblical principles will guide
you:

1. The "love of money" is wrong; that is, to value
material things above spiritual things; to accumulate
money for purely personal gain and advantage.

2. To obtain money in deceitful or dishonest ways
is a violation of God's laws.

3. To use money as a means for personal status
and power is a selfish use of material possessions.

4. Every Christian is to give regularly and propor-
tionally according to the way God has prospered him.

5. Christians are to use their material possessions
to care for other Christians who are in need.

6. Christians are not to be lazy and irresponsible,
living off of other people. This is sin.

# 16

# ONE WHO MANAGES HIS OWN HOUSEHOLD WELL

*An overseer, then, must be*
*above reproach, the husband of*
*one wife, temperate, prudent,*
*respectable, hospitable, able*
*to teach, not addicted to wine*
*or pugnacious, but gentle,*
*uncontentious, free from the*
*love of money.* **He must**
**be one who manages his own**
**household well,**
*keeping his children under control*
*with all dignity . . .*
*1 Timothy 3:2-4*

I once knew of a church where the main spiritual leader had a home that definitely did not measure up to Paul's specifications in 1 Timothy 3 and Titus 1. Two married daughters (both claiming to be Christians) committed adultery and one son was the town drunk. And yet this man continued to try to give directions to the church.

The results were disastrous. The church experienced continuous problems of disunity. There was lack of trust, gossiping, backbiting, and all sorts of carnality.

Interestingly, this man no doubt tried to handle the church problems the same way he handled his home problems. And the results were just the same. He often tried to ignore problems, to pretend they were not there (the old ostrich, head-in-the-sand approach). Or, when he could no longer avoid an issue, he would try to straddle the fence, not taking a stand. Though I am sure he had convictions, he would not exercise these convictions. Consequently, most everyone lost respect for him as a spiritual leader. By trying to please everyone, he pleased no one.

Thus Paul says in 1 Timothy 3:5: "But if a man does not know how to manage his own household, how will he take care of a church of God?"

The quality of being "one who manages his own household well" is probably the most significant mark of Christian maturity listed by Paul. It, above all others, reflects whether or not a man is above reproach, moral, temperate, prudent, respectable, etc. And it, more than any other single characteristic, demonstrates whether a man is mature enough to lead other Christians.

## WHAT PAUL DOESN'T MEAN!

To discover more specifically what Paul means by this quality of life, it is helpful to first of all discover what he *doesn't mean.*

First, he is not saying it is necessary to have children to be a spiritual leader in the church, nor to be a mature man of God.

I personally do not believe he is even saying an elder must be married. If this is what Paul meant, he would probably have been excluding himself since chances are he may never have been married himself. Rather it seems that Paul is simply saying that *if* a man is married, and *if* he has children, he is to have a well-ordered household. And of course, an additional implication is that *if* he does become a spiritual leader before he has a family, and then fails to measure up to Paul's criteria, he then would cease to be qualified to continue as a spiritual leader in the church.

Second, when Paul refers to the fact that a man must have "his children under control with all dignity," he is not referring here to small children.

There are several words used to describe children in the New Testament and the word Paul uses here and in Titus is a general word used for "offspring." This word, of course, *could* be used to refer to small children, but the total context in which Paul uses the word seems to indicate "grown" children.

Paul uses the same word in 1 Timothy chapter 5 when he talks about "mature children" who are responsible to provide for their mother's material needs (1 Tim. 5:4). Furthermore, in his letter to Titus, Paul specifies that a man chosen for a spiritual leadership position in the church must have children who believe, not accused of dissipation or "rebellion" (Titus 1:6). "Dissipation" and "rebellion" actually refer to riotous and improper living, characteristics that would be true only of older offspring.

An Old Testament example of a man who disqualified himself from spiritual leadership was Eli. Both of his sons as grown young men did "not know the Lord" (1 Sam. 2:12). They were both immoral and "they despised the offering of the Lord" (2:17). They were classified by God as "worthless" (2:12). Consequently, God judged *both* Eli and his sons. The reason? "Because his sons brought a curse on themselves and he [Eli] did not rebuke them" (3:13).

Third, since Paul is not referring here to small children, obviously he is not referring to the normal patterns of child growth and development.

Very small children particularly go through natural phases that have sometimes been superficially classified as the kind of "rebellion" Paul is referring to in Titus 1:7.

But there is also another very significant implication that needs emphasis. Some spiritual leaders come down too hard on their children for the sake of their own reputations. Or they try to get their teenagers particularly to conform to certain behavioral patterns in order that they, the spiritual leaders, are not criticized by other Christians in the church. Now, make no mistake! Children of Christian leaders should certainly be good examples. But they should be allowed to be "normal," both by parents and other Christians in the church. They resent a "higher standard" simply because their dad happens to be the pastor. And furthermore, they resent being told they are to "be good" so their dad "looks good." Ultimately this kind of motivation will backfire; even creating "rebellion" rather than "cooperation."

I like the approach of one pastor friend of mine. He overheard his son being reprimanded by another elder in the church. The elder who was criticizing his son said something like this: "I certainly would expect more from you than that, being the preacher's son." My friend—a gracious and mature Christian—immediately took the elder aside and, in no uncertain terms, let him know he never wanted that type of reprimand to happen again. Now understand! He was not defending his son. But he did not want his son to feel he was under some kind of "performance standard" just because he was the "preacher's kid."

"If my son is out of order," he said, "come to me and I'll discipline. Or if he needs immediate discipline and I am not available, don't use my position as a weapon against him."

Many Christian leaders and Christians generally could learn a good lesson from my friend.

Fourth, Paul is not speaking here of a man who has a perfect family.

There is no such thing. As there is no "perfect church," so there is no perfect family. There is no perfect husband or father, no perfect wife or mother, and certainly no perfect children. All Christians have problems in their family life. Satan will see to that. As long as we are in this world, we will be a victim of imperfection.

This does not mean, of course, that we should not strive towards having a family that is as free as possible from problems. But just as every Christian is in the process of becoming more and more like Jesus Christ, so should every family be in the process of growing spiritually.

Fifth, Paul is not talking primarily about how successful a man is in business.

Many people make the mistake of judging a man's capabilities for spiritual leadership on the basis of how well he runs his business; how efficient he is, how smart he is, and how much money he makes.

Now of course a man may have a "well-ordered family" *and* a "well-ordered business." Hopefully the two will be in alignment. And usually a man who manages his home well also manages his business well.

But the reverse is not always true. A man may have a "well-ordered business"—very well ordered, and yet he may have a family that is "falling apart."

The *family* is the true test! Some men through administrative skill and business acumen have become millionaires, but when it comes to family life, they are unable to communicate effectively with either their wives or children. Or they are too busy running their business, that they have not taken time to be good husbands and fathers. But in either case, they certainly would not pass the "spiritual maturity" test as laid out by Paul in his pastoral letters.

Sixth, Paul is not talking about how well a man can do church work.

Some pastors, missionaries, and lay leaders are well known for their achievements in Christian work. They have built large churches, led many to Jesus Christ, and are very active in the church. On the surface they appear to be very successful Christian leaders.

But what of their families? While ministering effectively to others many have neglected their own wives and children. In some instances their own sons and daughters grow up rejecting Jesus Christ and resenting Christian work because it has taken their parents away from them. Or on other occasions, children resent the hypocrisy they see in their parents. They know that they are preaching one thing in church and not living up to these truths in their homes.

It is very easy to fool other people regarding our

spirituality. But we *cannot* fool our wives and children. They live with us twenty-four hours a day, seven days a week. Their experience with us is "wall to wall." They know us as we really are. When our message does not conform to our "lives" we are in serious trouble with our children. And we are in danger of driving them away from Jesus Christ, the very One we want them to serve.

Unfortunately these people do not measure up to the mark of spiritual maturity spelled out by Paul. They are not qualified to be spiritual leaders, though they may be functioning in a spiritual leadership capacity. Though highly successful in Christian work, they do not have their own households in order. This, of course, is a tragedy.


## WHAT PAUL DOES MEAN

Paul viewed the well-ordered home as the true test of a man's maturity and ability to lead other Christians, especially a home that has passed the test of time. Where the whole household is committed to Jesus Christ and where you have a wife who is dedicated to her husband, and grown children particularly who respect and love their father, you have strong evidence that this man is spiritually and psychologically mature. He will certainly be able to "take care of the church of God" (1 Tim. 3:5).

But when this is not true, you are asking for serious problems in the church if a man is appointed as a spiritual leader. First, the very weakness that made him a poor husband and father will cause him to be a poor leader in the church. Second, if he accepts such a position, his family will have even less respect for him causing even greater problems in the home. In other words, we can make matters worse for his family by ignoring this important criterion for maturity.

## A GOAL FOR EVERY CHRISTIAN MAN

To be a good husband and father, to have a well-ordered household, should be a goal for every Christian man. All Christian husbands are to love their wives "just as Christ also loved the church" (Eph. 5:25). They are to live with them "in an understanding way" and to grant them "honor as a fellow-heir of the grace of life." Peter goes so far as to say that a man who does *not* live this way with his wife, will experience "unanswered prayer" (1 Peter 3:7).

Futhermore, fathers are *not* to provoke their children to anger but to "bring them up in the discipline and instruction of the Lord" (Eph. 6:4). And Paul elaborated on this concept with a personal illustration when he said he ministered among the Thessalonians like a "father would his own children," as he went about "exhorting and encouraging and imploring each one" (1 Thess. 2:11). This illustration, of course, shows how Paul viewed the father's responsibility to the children. He is not just to rear a family, but *individual children in that family,* "exhorting and encouraging and imploring each one."

The "father image" is an important concept in Scripture. And psychological studies help us understand *why*. Freud saw the implications, but drew false conclusions because he began with naturalistic presuppositions. He falsely concluded that the "god image" people have is a projection of the "father image," as a need for such a person. He saw it as a pure projection; that "God existed only in the minds of people."

But the truth is that man *does* develop certain ideas about God—the God who is actually there— because of various experiences with parents, fathers particularly. After all, we tell our children God is a *heavenly Father* and they quickly make a comparison. God, who is Spirit and invisible to a child, automatically takes on the same characteristics as an earthly father. Oftentimes if a father is kind and loving, so is God, in the mind of a child. At other times if Dad is cold and cruel, so is God in the mind of a child.

I'll never forget overhearing my daughters, when they were about ages four and five, having a discussion in the living room. Said one to the other: "You know, God is our heavenly daddy."

"Yours truly" was startled! I quickly realized that their "experience with me" was becoming their "experience with God." Needless to say, I was driven to a deeper commitment to exemplify Jesus Christ before my children, to help them develop a correct perspective mentally and emotionally, regarding God the Father.

## A PERSONAL PROJECT

The following project is designed to help you become a good husband and father: to have a "well-ordered household."

## Step A

Realize that you cannot demand or force respect and love. We must earn this kind of response by example and maturity.

## Step B

After reading over this material with your wife, have her help you evaluate your stature as a "husband" and "father." The following questions will guide you.

1. How can I become a better husband? What are my strengths? What are my weaknesses?

2. How can I become a better father? What are my strengths? What are my weaknesses?

3. In order to develop biblical goals for becoming a good husband and father, study the following questions and passages:

a. If I am to love my wife as Christ loved the church (Eph. 5:25), what attitudes and actions must I develop as outlined in Philippians 2:5-8?

b. If I am to become a good father, what must characterize my life, as outlined in Deuteronomy 6:4-9?

## Step C

If you have offended your wife and children in any way and have not been the example you should have been, ask them to forgive you.

## Step D

Set up specific goals for developing a "well-ordered household." Base these goals on actual needs you have surfaced through this study.

**SUGGESTION**

As you do, be sure to include your wife in your planning. Pray together about the needs you have surfaced. In some areas you will also want to include your children in helping you to set up goals. This will help to draw you together as a family. It is always easier to be a part of something when you have been a part of it in the planning stages.

# 17

## A GOOD REPUTATION WITH THOSE OUTSIDE

*And he must have **a good
reputation with those outside
the church**, so that he may
not fall into reproach and
the snare of the devil.*
*1 Timothy 3:7*

I had the privilege of growing up on a farm in In-
diana. One day, and I remember it as if it happened
yesterday, my father asked me to help another farmer
shell corn. Now "corn shelling" may not mean too
much to some of you, even those of you who are
familiar with the process. For the procedure today is
far different from those days. There were no picker-
shellers, and jet dryers, allowing a farmer to sell the
shelled corn to a local elevator within a week after
it had been harvested. Rather, in those days, corn
was picked, stored in a corn crib over winter (so it
would dry thoroughly), and then shelled in the spring.
Well, anyway, I was nominated in my family to help
a neighbor "shell out" his corn crib.

Now there were businessmen who made their live-
lihood by operating corn shellers. The huge machine
was mounted on the back of a truck, allowing the

owner to back up to a crib and shell the farmers' corn. My job? To rake the corn into the sheller! As I was performing my task, I began to share Jesus Christ with the fellow who owned the sheller. You see, at the age of sixteen I had just become a Christian, and the young man standing next to me—oh, a few years older—was in the same Sunday School class as I was. And I knew he was not a Christian.

I had only gotten started with my personal testimony when he stopped me short with a jolting statement! His conflict was not with me, but with *our* Sunday School teacher. It seems that the man who taught us had engaged in some bad business practice, involving this same young man. I'll never forget his charge.

"Do you think," he asked, "that that man is going to heaven and me to hell when I live a better life than he does?"

Here was an older man who was a Christian and a Bible teacher, but who had a "bad reputation" in business. Though a stumbling block to this young non-Christian businessman who owned the corn sheller, it became a dynamic lesson to me as a new and growing Christian! How important it is to have "a good reputation with those outside the church." It is, without doubt, one of the most significant marks of spiritual maturity! And with *this* the apostle Paul would agree, as well as other inspired writers of Scripture.

## A GOOD REPUTATION

A number of passages of Scripture speak decisively regarding the importance of *all believers* having a good reputation among non-Christians. Consider the following rather clear-cut statements:

". . . Make it your ambition to lead a quiet life and attend to your own business and work with your hands, just as we commanded you; so that you may behave properly toward outsiders and not be in any need" (1 Thess. 4:11,12).

"Conduct yourselves with wisdom toward outsiders, making the most of the opportunity. Let your speech always be with grace, seasoned, as it were, with salt, so that you may know how you should respond to each person" (Col. 4:5,6).

"Whether, then, you eat or drink or whatever you do, do all to the glory of God. Give no offense either to Jews or to Greeks or to the church of God; just as I also please all men in all things, not seeking my own profit, but the profit of the many, that they may be saved" (1 Cor. 10:31-33).

"Keep your behavior excellent among the Gentiles, so that in the thing in which they slander you as evildoers, they may on account of your good deeds as they observe them, glorify God in the day of visitation" (1 Pet. 2:12).

There is no doubt as you read these passages of Scripture that it is God's will for a Christian to have a "good reputation" before the unsaved world. Any Christian who fails to measure up to this criterion should not be appointed as a spiritual leader in the church. If we make such an appointment, we are not only creating problems for the body of Christ, but also for the man himself.

## SO "THAT HE MAY NOT FALL INTO REPROACH"

To "fall into reproach" means to be criticized or blamed for something. A Christian who is reproached by a non-Christian is under attack and he is being faulted for something the unbeliever dislikes.

The Bible, however, presents two perspectives on the concept of "being reproached." On the one hand it deals with the inevitability and even the "blessedness" of a Christian being "reproached." On the other hand, as in 1 Timothy 3:7, it deals with the inappropriateness of "being reproached." How can these two ideas be reconciled?

### A Positive Perspective

Jesus Himself spoke of the positive aspects of being reproached. As He shared the Beatitudes with the multitudes, He said: "Blessed are you when men revile you [reproach you], and say all kinds of evil against you falsely, on account of Me" (Matt. 5:11; Luke 6:22).

The apostle Peter shares the same concept with the Christians "scattered throughout" the New Testament world. "If you are reviled (reproached) for the name of Christ," he wrote in his first epistle, "you are blessed, because the Spirit of glory and of God rests upon you" (1 Pet. 4:14). And Paul adds, "And indeed, all who desire to live godly in Christ Jesus will be persecuted" (2 Tim. 3:12).

Christians, therefore, should not be surprised when they are reproached by non-Christians (1 John 3:13). In particular situations and under certain circumstances, it *will happen*. Certain convictions and attitudes will bring a negative response. Since they also hated Jesus, we should not be suprised if they hate us (John 15:18-20).

What, then, is Paul speaking of in 1 Timothy 3?

## A Negative Perspective

Though "reproach" from non-Christians often accompanies a *godly* life-style, particularly in a culture that represses Christianity, it should never result from *ungodly* behavior. After reminding Christians that it is "blessed" to be "reviled for the name of Christ," Peter warns: "By no means let any of you suffer as a murderer, or thief, or evil-doer, or a troublesome meddler." This is only to ask for trouble. And it hurts the whole body of Christ. This is reproach that comes from non-Christian behavior, from a poor testimony, and from a bad reputation. This, then, is what Paul is talking about in 1 Timothy 3.

## THE SNARE OF THE DEVIL

In 1 Timothy 3:7 Paul cautions against appointing a man to a position as elder and spiritual leader in the church who has a bad reputation with non-Christians. If you do, he says, this mark of immaturity may cause him to "fall into reproach and the snare of the devil."

A snare is a trap or a noose. Paul uses the same word later in his first letter to Timothy when he talks about riches. "But those," he says, "who want to get rich fall into temptation and a snare and many foolish and hurtful desires which plunge men into ruin and destruction" (1 Tim. 6:9). And in his second letter to Timothy, Paul gives instructions on how to help people "come to their senses and escape from the snare of the devil, having been held captive by him to do his will" (2 Tim. 2:26).

How then does being "reproached" by non-Christians for immature Christian behavior lead to being caught in the devil's trap? Though it is difficult to pinpoint exactly what Paul had in mind, the Scriptures give us several clues.

### Shame

Reproach can cause a man to feel terribly "put down," "crushed," embarrassed and intensely guilty. In the same passage referred to in 1 Peter, the apostle says: "By no means let any of you suffer as a murderer, or thief, or evil-doer, or a troublesome meddler; but if anyone suffers as a Christian, let him not feel ashamed, but in that name let him glorify God" (1 Pet. 4:15,16).

Here Peter is encouraging the Christians who are being reproached for "righteousness' sake" to take heart and not to feel guilty or embarrassed. Obviously if a Christian who has *no* reason to be ashamed, actually *feels* ashamed, then the Christian who is reproached for bad behavior will have *double reason* to "be ashamed."

This can be a "snare of the devil." The kind of emotion described here can lead a man to persistent depression, physical sickness, and almost total despair. Thus when Paul wrote to the Corinthians, he urged them to restore the one they had disciplined, lest he be "overwhelmed by excessive sorrow" (2 Cor.

171

2:7). Interestingly this man was engaging in sin that was not even approved by the unsaved (1 Cor. 5:1).

A state of sorrow and despair gives the devil an opportunity to accomplish many goals, both in the life of the one who has failed, and also in the lives of other people, Christians and non-Christians alike. It is also important to note that "failure as a Christian" is somewhat different from "failure as a Christian leader." To fail as a spiritual leader and to be reproached by nonbelievers for bad behavior is also to fail other members of the body of Christ, and to be brought under their judgment as well. "Don't," said Paul, "put a man with this kind of immaturity in a spiritual leadership role, for he will surely fall into the devil's trap when he is criticized by non-Christians."

### Fear and Loss of Confidence

It is a natural tendency to withdraw, to retreat, and to shrink back when attacked by *anyone*. Even Paul, the great apostle, experienced fear and emotional conflict when reproached both verbally and physically by unsympathetic people (2 Cor. 7:5,6). Consequently, the writer to the Hebrews warns those New Testament Christians—those Christians particularly who had been publicly embarrassed, who had even lost their property. "Do not," he says, "throw away your confidence," your courage, your boldness, your assurance. Putting it in the vernacular, the writer to those Hebrew Christians is saying "hang in there" because you are doing "the will of God." And if you endure, you will be rewarded (Heb. 10:36).

Again, if fear and loss of self-confidence is a nat-

172

ural tendency for all people who are reproached, how much more so for the immature, sinning Christian. A guilty and embarrassed believer is a real candidate for withdrawal and retreat. Satan's trap is just waiting to spring on a discouraged Christian.

## Anger and Defensiveness

There is also another natural reaction to reproach. It's retaliation. Thus Paul warns the Roman Christians: "Never pay back evil for evil to anyone. . . . Never take your own revenge. . . . Do not be overcome by evil, but overcome evil with good" (Rom. 12:17,19,21).

It is easy to fight back, to defend oneself, especially when innocent, but it is *even easier* to fight back when guilty. A guilty person is a defensive person.

It should be noted at this juncture that it is possible to be angry as a Christian and yet not to sin (Eph. 4:26). But it is also possible to "let the sun go down" on our anger, and when we do, says Paul, we are going to give "the devil an opportunity" (Eph. 4:27).

Obviously an immature Christian is extremely vulnerable to anger; especially one whose behavior is being reproached by non-Christians. In fact, this may be his first response before he eventually feels shame, guilt, despair, and loss of self-confidence. In his attempt to save face as a spiritual leader, he may rationalize, attempt to justify himself and retaliate. When he does, the devil has his trap set; this is his big opportunity. For as with Cain, initial anger and a wounded ego and feelings of rejection led eventually to even greater sin—in this case murder!

## A PERSONAL PROJECT

The following project is designed to help you develop a good reputation with non-Christians.

### Step A

Test your behavior according to Scripture. Read the following questions and Scripture passages. Be honest! How do you measure up?

*Check* the specific *questions* where you feel you have failed. Also circle specific scriptural statements where you sensed that you have fallen short of God's standard.

☐ Do I do *all things* without grumbling and disputing?

"Do all things without grumbling and disputing; that you may prove yourselves to be blameless and innocent, children of God above reproach in the midst of a crooked and perverse generation, among whom you appear as lights in the world, holding fast the word of life, so that in the day of Christ I may have cause to glory because I did not run in vain nor toil in vain" (Phil. 2:14-16).

☐ Am I above reproach in my business life?

"Make it your ambition to lead a quiet life and attend to your business and work with your own hands, just as we commanded you; so that you may behave properly toward outsiders and not be in any need" (1 Thess. 4:11,12).

☐ Do I conduct my affairs in a wise way, being cautious about both my speech and my conduct?

"Conduct yourselves with wisdom toward outsiders, making the most of the opportunity. Let your

174

speech always be with grace, seasoned, as it were, with salt, so that you may know how you should respond to each person" (Col. 4:5,6).

☐ Is my social life a good testimony before non-Christians?

"Whether, then, you eat or drink or whatever you do, do all to the glory of God. Give no offense either to Jews or to Greeks or to the church of God; just as I also please all men and all things, not seeking my own profit, but the profit of the many, that they may be saved" (1 Cor. 10:31-33).

☐ Do I show respect to my non-Christian employer or employees?

"Slaves, be obedient to those who are your masters according to the flesh, with fear and trembling, in the sincerity of your heart, as to Christ; not by way of eyeservice, as men-pleasers, but as slaves of Christ, doing the will of God from the heart. With good will render service, as to the Lord, and not to men, knowing that whatever good thing each one does, this he will receive back from the Lord, whether slave or free. And, masters, do the same things to them, and give up threatening, knowing that both their Master and yours is in heaven, and there is no partiality with Him" (Eph. 6:5-9).

☐ Do I live a consistent and exemplary life, even when I'm falsely accused?

"Keep your behavior excellent among the Gentiles, so that in the thing in which they slander you as evildoers, they may on account of your good deeds, as they observe them, glorify God in the day of visitation" (1 Pet. 2:12).

## Step B

Take specific steps of action in areas of your life where you are weak. Following are some questions that will help you do this. Pinpoint *your* needs.

1. Have you settled these matters with God?

2. Have you made amends when your behavior toward non-Christians has hurt other members of the body of Christ?

3. Is an apology necessary to your unsaved neighbor? To your employer? To your employees?

4. What goals do you need to set up regarding your future behavior?

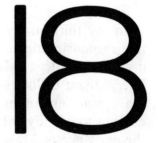

# LOVING WHAT IS GOOD

*For the overseer must be*
*above reproach as God's steward,*
*not self-willed,*
*not quick-tempered,*
*not addicted to wine,*
*not pugnacious,*
*not fond of sordid gain,*
*but hospitable,*
***loving what is good*** *. . .*
*Titus 1:7,8*


In my thirteen years of teaching and administrative responsibilities at Moody Bible Institute, it was my great privilege to learn to know quite well the late Dr. William Culbertson, who served as president of that great institution for many years. Before ever coming to Moody Bible Institute, Dr. Culbertson, at the early age of 21, was elected to serve as bishop of the New York and Philadelphia Synod of the Reformed Episcopal Church, a distinct tribute, for he was the youngest man ever elected to serve in this position. Among those who knew Dr. Culbertson well, both fellow workers and students, there was one common statement used to describe him. "He is," they would often say, "a man of God." As I personally reflected on the characteristic or mark of Christian maturity before us—"loving what is good"

—my thoughts went back immediately to my associations with this man. "There was a man," I thought, "who, without doubt, *loved what is good!*"

## GOOD VERSUS EVIL

To "love what is good" means to desire to *do* good, not evil. Interestingly, this is the contrast that appears frequently in Scripture. We are not, said Paul, to "be overcome by evil," but we are to "overcome evil with good" (Rom. 12:21). And in describing his own inner struggles, when his flesh dominated and controlled him, Paul says: "For the good that I wish, I do not do; but I practice the very evil that I do not wish" (Rom. 7:19).

And again Paul says, writing to the Corinthian Christians, "For we must all appear before the judgment seat of Christ, that each one may be recompensed for his deeds in the body, according to what he has done, whether good or bad" (2 Cor. 5:10).

A number of words can be used to describe what the New Testament classifies as *good*. It is that which is useful, salutary, pleasant, agreeable, excellent, upright and honorable. Perhaps it can be best summarized with one of Paul's closing exhortations to the Philippian Christians: "Finally, brethren, whatever is true, honorable, whatever is right, whatever is pure, whatever is lovely, whatever is of good repute, if there is any excellence and if anything worthy of praise, let your mind dwell on these things" (Phil. 4:8).

By contrast the Scriptures spell out *evil* desires and activities. In discussing the "man who does evil,"

Paul talks about "those who are selfishly ambitious" and those who "do not obey the truth, but obey unrighteousness . . ." (Rom. 2:8,9).

To the Ephesians Paul wrote: "Let no unwholesome word proceed from your mouth, but only such a word as is good for edification . . ." (Eph. 4:29).

And in writing to Titus, Paul put it all together, when he says: "To the pure all things are pure; but to those who are defiled and unbelieving, nothing is pure, but both their mind and their conscience are defiled. They profess to know God, but by their deeds they deny Him, being detestable and disobedient, and worthless for any good deed" (Titus 1:15,16).

## SCRIPTURAL PREREQUISITES FOR DOING GOOD

To "love what is good"—and to "do what is good" is not automatic. It is part of the process of becoming mature, of becoming more and more like Jesus Christ. True, "we are His workmanship, created in Christ Jesus for good works" but to "walk in them" is another story (Eph. 2:10). It is only as we determine to "do good to all men" (Gal. 6:10), and then draw upon God's resources that we will be able to carry out God's will.

### An Act of Commitment

The Bible makes it very clear how Christians can "prove what the will of God is, that which is good and acceptable and perfect" (Rom. 12:1,2). You must "present your bodies a living and holy sacrifice," says Paul. You must "not be conformed to this

180

world, but be transformed by the renewing of your mind." This is an act of our will. It involves determination. God doesn't demand it, but He urges us to do it, even begs us to do it. And His appeal is based on what He has done for us—His marvelous grace— "the mercies of God" which was manifested to us by sending Jesus Christ to be a sacrifice for our sins (Rom. 12:1).

A man who learns to "love what is good" must first of all be a man who loves God, for God is good. He must be a man who turns everything over to God and desires to walk consistently and day by day in His will.

## A Knowledge of God's Word

When Paul wrote to Timothy, a young New Testament pastor, he urged him to continue to practice the Word of God in his life; to "continue in the things" he had "learned and become convinced of . . ." (2 Tim. 3:14). Paul was talking, of course, about "the sacred writings"—the holy Scriptures (3:15). "All Scripture," continued Paul, "is inspired of God and profitable for teaching, for reproof, for correction, for training in righteousness; that the man of God might be adequate, equipped for every good work" (3:16,17).

A man who learns to "love what is good" must then, first, love God and desire to do His will. And second, he must love God's Word and seek to know His will through its inspired teaching.

## Prayer for Godly Wisdom

It is one thing to love God, and to love and know

His Word, but it is yet another matter to apply the Scriptures in a wise and understanding way.

Paul's prayer for the Colossians is unique in this respect: "For this reason also, since the day we heard of it, we have not ceased to pray for you and to ask that you may be filled with the knowledge of His will in all spiritual wisdom and understanding, so that you may walk in a manner worthy of the Lord, to please Him in all respects, bearing fruit in every good work" (Col. 1:9,10).

James too speaks of this wisdom. He calls it "wisdom from above" which, he says, "is first pure, then peaceable, gentle, reasonable, full of mercy and good fruits, unwavering, without hypocrisy" (Jas. 3:17). And if you want it, you can have it, says James. For, "if any of you lacks wisdom, let him ask of God, who gives to all men generously and without reproach, and it will be given to him" (Jas. 1:5).

Prayer then is the key that unlocks the Word of God and opens our eyes and our hearts to the Spirit of God, enabling us to not only "love what is good" but enabling us to apply the Word of God in a wise and understanding way.


## A PERSONAL PROJECT

This personal project is designed to help you "love what is good."


### Step A

Realize that to "love what is good" is more than *contemplation,* it is *action.* It is something you *do.* Note again 2 Corinthians 5:10.

"For we must all appear before the judgment seat of Christ, that each one may be recompensed for his deeds in the body, according to what he has done, whether good or bad."

## Step B

Evaluate your actions by scriptural criteria. Are you *practicing* the following biblical directives in your daily life?

1. Do I take advantage of opportunities to do good to *all* men—both Christians and non-Christians?

"So then, while we have opportunity, let us do good to all men, and especially to those who are of the household of faith" (Gal. 6:10).

"Remind them to be subject to rulers, to authorities, to be obedient, to be ready for every good deed, to malign no one, to be uncontentious, gentle, showing every consideration for all men" (Titus 3:1,2).

2. Do I build people up, or tear them down?

"Let no unwholesome word proceed from your mouth, but only such a word as is good for edification according to the need of the moment, that it may give grace to those who hear" (Eph. 4:29).

3. Am I using my material resources to help others in need?

"Now this I say, he who sows sparingly shall also reap sparingly; and he who sows bountifully shall also reap bountifully. Let each one do just as he has purposed in his heart; not grudgingly or under compulsion; for God loves a cheerful giver. And God is able to make all grace abound to you, that always having all sufficiency in everything, you may have an abundance for every good deed" (2 Cor. 9:6-8).

4. Do I have a good conscience about my behavior?

"This command I entrust to you, Timothy, my son, in accordance with the prophecies previously made concerning you, that by them you may fight the good fight, keeping faith and a good conscience, which some have rejected and suffered shipwreck in regard to their faith" (1 Tim. 1:18,19).

5. Am I truly concerned about the unity of the body of Christ, or am I jealous, selfish and proud, creating tension and lack of harmony?

"Who among you is wise and understanding? Let him show by his good behavior his deeds in the gentleness of wisdom. But if you have bitter jealousy and selfish ambition in your heart, do not be arrogant and so lie against the truth. This wisdom is not that which comes down from above, but is earthly, natural, demonic. For where jealousy and selfish ambition exist, there is disorder and every evil thing. But the wisdom from above is first pure, then peaceable, gentle, reasonable, full of mercy and good fruits, unwavering, without hypocrisy" (Jas. 3:13-17).

"To sum up, let all be harmonious, sympathetic, brotherly, kind-hearted, and humble in spirit; not returning evil for evil, or insult for insult, but giving a blessing instead; for you are called for the very purpose that you might inherit a blessing. . . . And let him turn away from evil and do good; let him seek peace and pursue it" (1 Pet. 3:8,9,11).

## Step C
Evaluate your Christian commitment in the light of Romans 12:1 and 2. Have you truly presented

your *total life* to Jesus Christ without reservations? It is only as you do so that you can discover day by day God's will "which is good and acceptable and perfect." Read the verses which follow and then do what they say. Note that to *present your body* is a once-for-all event. To *renew your mind* is a process of becoming more and more like Jesus Christ.

"I urge you therefore, brethren, by the mercies of God, to present your bodies a living and holy sacrifice, acceptable to God, which is your spiritual service of worship. And do not be conformed to this world, but be ye transformed by the renewing of your mind, that you may prove what the will of God is, that which is good and acceptable and perfect."

## Step D

Now that you have done *your* part, trust God to do *His.* Claim the following promises: "For I am confident of this very thing, that He who began a good work in you will perfect it until the day of Jesus Christ" (Phil. 1:6).

"Now the God of peace, who brought up from the dead the great Shepherd of the sheep through the blood of the eternal covenant, even Jesus our Lord, equip you in every good thing to do his will, working in us that which is pleasing in His sight, through Jesus Christ; to whom be the glory for ever and ever. Amen" (Heb. 13:20,21).

JUST

*For the overseer*
*must be above reproach*
*as God's steward,*
*not self-willed,*
*not quick-tempered,*
*not addicted to wine,*
*not pugnacious,*
*not fond of sordid gain,*
*but hospitable, loving what*
*is good, sensible, **just** . . .*
*Titus 1:7,8*

The word *"just"* (*dikaios*) in the New Testament is translated in various ways and is used to mean different things. For example, the Bible refers to the "just and the unjust," obviously referring to those who are saved and unsaved (Acts 24:15; Matt. 9:13; 13:24-30). Paul says the "righteous [just] man shall live by faith" (Rom. 1:17), again referring to God's justifying work in the life of a sinner who, by faith is made righteous in God's sight. This is *positional righteousness*.

The Bible also uses the word "just" to refer to *practical righteousness*—a man who is living a godly and righteous life. For example, in the *King James Version* Joseph is spoken of as being a "just man"

(Matt. 1:19). So is Cornelius (Acts 10:22). And Herod was afraid of John the Baptist, because he knew "that he was a righteous [just] and holy man" (Mark 6:20).

But there seems to be a more specific *application* of the word *just* in Scripture. Although *dikaios* is no doubt referring to proper Christian behavior and practical righteousness, and is inseparably linked to *hosios* (the next quality listed in Titus 1:18), the word can certainly be related to the quality of *prudence* (see chapter 5). In other words, a just and righteous man is also wise and discerning, able to make mature and proper judgments in his relationships with others.

## SOME BIBLICAL EXAMPLES

### The Corinthians

When writing to the Corinthians, Paul chided these immature Christians because they could not settle certain problems having to do with lawsuits against each other. They were going to pagan law courts to try to resolve their conflicts. Paul was upset with them. "I say this to your shame," he exclaimed. "Is it so, that there is not among you one wise man who will be able to decide between his brethren . . . ?" (1 Cor. 6:1-5). This is perhaps why there is no reference to elders in Paul's letters to the Corinthians. The church was made up of so many psychologically and spiritually immature Christians that it seems that no one was qualified to be a spiritual leader (1 Cor. 3:1-3).

A just man, then, as Paul uses the word in Titus 1:8, is one who can make mature judgments. He has a mature viewpoint on life and its many variables and circumstances. He is a man of wisdom and understanding (Prov. 1:1-6).

## Solomon

In the Old Testament, Solomon, of course, stands out as one of the wisest men who ever lived. When God asked him what he desired, he humbly prayed for "an understanding heart to judge Thy people to discern between good and evil" (1 Kings 3:5-9). God was pleased with Solomon's sincere and unselfish prayer. Consequently, God granted his request. "Behold," said the Lord, "I have given you a wise and discerning heart, so that there has been no one like you before you, nor shall one like you arise after you" (3:10-12). And Solomon amazed his people and the nations around him with his wisdom and his justice (3:28).

Unfortunately Solomon did not stay close to God, walking in His ways and doing His will. Consequently, like so many Old Testament leaders, he later sinned greatly and suffered the consequences. This is a significant Old Testament lesson for all Christians. In the very context of referring to Old Testament examples for New Testament Christians, Paul warns: "Therefore let him who thinks he stands take heed lest he fall" (1 Cor. 10:12). These words of Paul reflect his own concern about his life. In another place Paul writes that he was constantly on guard so that he, after having preached to others, would not fail (1 Cor. 9:27).

## Daniel

Daniel is an exceptional Old Testament example. He had a good beginning, a faithful and God-fearing life, and a noble and praiseworthy ending. He put God first in his life, kept Him there, and was used greatly by the Lord. Even as a very young man, he served as a consultant to the king of Babylon. And of him it was said (along with his three friends): "And as for every matter of wisdom and understanding about which the king consulted them, he found them ten times better than all the magicians and conjurers who were in all his realm" (Dan. 1:20).

There was a reason for this. Daniel had "made up his mind" that he would please and serve God (Dan. 1:8). And no matter what happened—even living day by day in the midst of raw paganism—he, unlike Solomon, was not sidetracked into its way of life.

His attitudes toward prayer and worship are an unparalleled example of his unbending commitment and devotion to God. Even when his life was threatened, he continued to worship the God of heaven. In full view of those who set an insidious trap for him, he knelt and prayed three times a day (Daniel 6), and because of his commitment to God, he was miraculously saved from a horrible death in the lions' pit.

The point is, of course, that Daniel was a dedicated child of God. Come what may, his commitment to God was first. He maintained a proper perspective on life. His judgments were wise and discerning ones, again and again putting him in a prominent place in the Babylonian kingdom.

## DEVELOPING A MATURE VIEWPOINT

How can a man become wise and just? Two things must be true. This type of behavior calls for both *spiritual* and *psychological* maturity.

Interestingly the non-Christian man can have one without the other. A person does not have to be a believer to be a *just* man, in the sense of making wise and discerning judgments in many areas of life's problems. Obviously, as a non-Christian, a man is not spiritually mature, but his depth of emotional stability and his keen and discerning mind may enable him to make mature and fair decisions. Consider the many non-Christian judges and leaders who demonstrate this ability every day. (There are notable exceptions, of course.)

Earlier we referred to Daniel! He was a wise and just man, *and* a man of God. But the Bible says that there was a pagan man in Old Testament days who was even wiser than Daniel. He was the ruler or prince of Tyre, and God says through Ezekiel: "Behold, you [the prince of Tyre] are wiser than Daniel; there is no secret that is a match for you. By your wisdom and understanding you have acquired riches for yourself . . ." (Ezek. 28:3,4).

On one occasion Jesus stated that the "sons of this age are more shrewd [wise] in relation to their own kind than the sons of light" (Luke 16:8), and later He referred to a wise decision by an unrighteous judge to illustrate the attitude of God toward His children (Luke 18:1-8).[1]

But note! A man can never be a mature leader in the church without *both* spiritual and psychological maturity. There is no spiritual maturity without psychological maturity. In fact psychological maturity appears to be a prerequisite to spiritual maturity.

It is important to note that a man's *relationship* or *fellowship* with God is not the issue here. It is possible to be in tune with God spiritually, and yet to be an immature Christian psychologically and spiritually. There may be no open and conscious sin in a man's life and yet when measured against the criteria for maturity in 1 Timothy and Titus, he may be woefully lacking.

In actuality, a wise man who is just and fair must also reflect most of the other qualifications of leadership listed by Paul. In fact they are prerequisites to this quality of justness and, consequently, all of these qualities must be developed concurrently with the quality of being just. *Some* of the qualities, however, correlate in a significant way with the quality of being "just" and have a particular relationship to psychological maturity. They are: being *temperate, prudent, able to teach, gentle; not self-willed, not quick-tempered, not pugnacious and uncontentious.*

A Christian leader, however, must have more than psychological maturity. Closely aligned and interrelated with the above are the qualities that have a particular relationship to spiritual maturity: above reproach (with both Christians and non-Christians), husband of one wife, not given to wine, free from the love of money, love what is good, and a quality yet to be developed in the section to follow—devout.


## A PERSONAL PROJECT
This personal project is designed to help you de-

velop the quality of being just—to make wise and mature decisions and judgments.

## Step A

Develop your prayer life in this area. James says: "If any of you lacks wisdom, let him ask of God, who gives to all men generously and without reproach, and it will be given to him. But let him ask in faith without any doubting . . ." (Jas. 1:5,6).

## Step B

Review all of the previous projects. How well have you done? What steps have you taken? If you have made satisfactory progress in your life, you are well on your way to developing a psychological and spiritual maturity that will almost automatically reflect the quality of being just. If you have not made satisfactory progress, you will have difficulty being just. For example, if you are still unusually insecure and lack self-confidence, you will no doubt make bad judgments when dealing with people. Threatened people become emotional, which affects the clarity of their thinking.

Evaluate your maturity level! At this point you may need to back up and work on some weak areas in your life before you can proceed further.

## Step C

No matter whatever your progress, you need to continue to develop the quality of being just. Realizing that no man in this life can reach perfection, we must continue to become more and more conformed to the image of Jesus Christ. Here, then, are some practical suggestions for developing this quality even more:

1. Look for opportunities to observe wise men in action. Learn from their successes as well as their failures.

*Note:* There are many opportunities for making this kind of observation, even outside of being involved in a closed circle of leaders. For example, observe mature men in action. What makes them successful in their relatonships with people? Observe immature men in action. What makes them unsuccessful in their relationships with people? You can learn from both their successes and failures.

2. Learn to use other mature members of the body of Christ to test your judgments. Don't be proud! Be open to suggestions and correction. There is security in numbers. "Where there is no guidance, the people fall, but in abundance of counselors there is victory" (Prov. 11:14).

3. Admit it when you have made a bad judgment. But don't dwell on it! Do what you can to correct the problem and learn from your failure.

*Remember:* There is a fine line between success and failure. Don't let failure get you down! Remember the words of Paul who said, "Not that I have already attained it, or have already become perfect, but I press on in order that I may lay hold of that for which also I was laid hold of by Jesus Christ. Brethren, I do not regard myself as having laid hold of it yet; but one thing I do: forgetting what lies behind and reaching forward to what lies ahead, I press on toward the goal for the prize of the upward call of God in Christ Jesus" (Phil. 3:12-14).

1. This term "unjust" in Luke 18 in the Authorized Version means "unrighteous," not "unwise." This man, though ungodly, evidently was a wise man. At least Jesus thought highly enough of his decision to use it as an illustration of God's attitude toward His own people.

20

DEVOUT

*For the overseer
must be above reproach as
God's steward, not self-willed,
not quick-tempered,
not addicted to wine,
not pugnacious,
not fond of sordid gain,
but hospitable,
loving what is good,
sensible, just, **devout** . . .
Titus 1:7,8*

The word "devout" like *just,* refers to *practical holiness.* The word in the original is *hosios.* It means to be free from sin or wickedness. The *Authorized Version* actually uses the word "holy." Another word that is frequently translated "holy" in the New Testament is the word *hagios.* It refers primarily to *positional holiness;* that is, to be "set apart for God." In the Old Testament God spoke of the children of Israel as being a "holy nation"; that is, a "nation set apart." Obviously, they were not always *holy* in actuality. They were far from it, but they did not cease to be a "holy nation" or a "nation set apart."

In the New Testament God also speaks of the body of Christ as being a "holy people"; that is, a group of people that have been chosen by God and set apart (Eph. 2:21). And just as the children of

Israel on many occasions did not measure up to their calling, Christians often do not measure up to their calling in Christ. Consequently, Paul had to exhort believers to "walk in a manner worthy of the calling" with which they had been called (Eph. 4:1).

When Paul talks about a man who is "devout" in Titus 1:8, he is therefore speaking of an attitude of holiness that is developed and worked out in human behavior. It is not "imputed holiness" but "progressive holiness." It is that quality that shows that a believer is in the process of becoming like Jesus Christ in his daily life and behavior. Following are some specific references in the New Testament to this kind of life-style.

## CHRIST'S EXAMPLE

In Hebrews 7:26 Jesus Christ is presented as the "high priest . . . holy, innocent, undefiled, separated from sinners. . . ." Here, as in Titus 1:8, the word translated holy is *hosios,* referring to observable, practical holiness.

Note also the additional words which are used to describe Christ's life-style and which immediately follow the word "holy." Christ was also *innocent*— that is, He was free from being crafty and having malice in his heart. He was *undefiled*—that is, He was not tainted by sin. And He was *separated from sinners*—that is, He did not participate in their evil deeds.

A word needs to be said about Christ's "separation from sinners." Some have interpreted Christian separation as withdrawing and separating from any contact with sinners in order to be holy. This is a perversion of the Word of God and certainly of Christ's life-style. This is isolation, not separation. Jesus Christ frequently associated with tax-gatherers and sinners. He even ate with them (Matt. 9:9-12), and when the Pharisees asked *why* He was associating with such men, Christ Himself responded by saying: "It is not those who are healthy who need a physician, but those who are ill."

With this example, Christ is illustrating for all Christians that it is possible to live a holy and devout life in the midst of sinful humanity. To be with them does not mean we have to be like them.

Paul too was misinterpreted regarding this concept of separation. On one occasion when he wrote to the Corinthians, he told them not to associate with immoral people, that is, people who claimed to be Christians and continued to live in sin. The Corinthians thought he meant *all* immoral people. Consequently Paul had to correct this false concept: "I wrote to you in my letter," he said, "not to associate with immoral people; I did not at all mean with the immoral people of this world, or with the covetous and swindlers, or with idolators; for then you would actually have to go out of the world" (1 Cor. 5:9,10).

It is possible then to "be in this world" without "being a part of it." It is possible to be "set apart" for God without being "set aside" from those who do not know Christ.

Christians are to be the "salt of the earth" and the "light of the world" (Matt. 5:13,14). Living a *holy* and righteous life in the midst of those who are unbelievers (as Christ did) illustrates salt that has not lost its taste, and light that is not hid under a bushel. In the words of Jesus Christ Himself, "Let your light shine before men in such a way that they may see your good works, and glorify your Father who is in heaven" (Matt. 5:16).

## PAUL'S EXAMPLE

The apostle Paul's own life-style also illustrates what he meant when he listed "devout" as a mark of Christian maturity in Titus 1:8. When writing his first letter to the Thessalonian Christians, in which he reflected upon his own behavior among these people, he had this to say: "You are witnesses, and so is God, how devoutly [holily] and uprightly and blamelessly we behaved toward you believers" (1 Thess. 2:10).

Here again is *practical* holiness. It was observable behavior. The Thessalonians were a witness to Paul's godly life-style and so was God. And as with Christ's example in Hebrews 7:16, several words are used to describe this life-style. We also lived "uprightly," reflected Paul; that is, we lived according to God's norm—His law. And we also lived "blamelessly"; that is, above reproach. Together, the words *devoutly, uprightly* and *blamelessly* form a powerful Christian witness, spoken of a life that reflected the holiness and righteousness of Jesus Christ. And no one who knew the facts firsthand could deny it. This is why Paul could write to the Corinthians and say: "Be imitators of me, just as I also am of Christ" (1 Cor. 11:1).[1]

## AN EXHORTATION FOR EVERY BELIEVER

In Paul's letter to the Ephesians, Paul reminds us once again that the marks of maturity specified for elders in 1 Timothy 3 and Titus 1 are actually goals for every believer. "Put on the new self," he wrote, "which, in the likeness of God has been created in righteousness and holiness of the truth" (Eph. 4:24). Here again is practical holiness—not *positional*. Contextually, Paul is writing about the Christian's walk, his day-by-day and moment-by-moment life-style (Eph. 4:17).

The key word in this Ephesian passage is "learn" (4:20). Following an enumeration of those qualities that characterized a pagan life-style (4:17-19)—a futile mind, darkened understanding, alienation from God, ignorance, hardness of heart, sensuality, impurity and greed—Paul then states emphatically: "But you did not learn Christ in this way!" (4:20). In other words, this kind of holiness must be *learned* from the very life-style of Christ Himself.

And what is this life-style? After exhorting the Ephesian Christians to "lay aside the old self" (4:22) and to "put on the new self" which is characterized by righteousness and holiness (4:24), Paul then spells out in detail what he means by a life-style of holiness, and by far the most significant and comprehensive commentary on the word "devout" which he uses in Titus 1:8. Following are some of Paul's specific exhortations in order to live a devout or holy life:

☐ "Laying aside falsehood, speak truth, each one of you with his neighbor" (4:25).

202

☐ "Be angry, and yet do not sin; do not let the sun go down on your anger" (4:26).

☐ "Let him who steals steal no longer; but rather let him labor, performing with his own hands what is good" (4:28).

☐ "Let no unwholesome word proceed from your mouth, but only such a word as is good for edification" (4:29).

☐ "Do not grieve the Holy Spirit of God" (4:30).

☐ "Let all bitterness and wrath and anger and clamor and slander be put away from you, along with all malice" (4:31).

☐ "Be kind to one another, tender-hearted, forgiving each other" (4:32).

☐ "Walk in love, just as Christ also loved you" (5:2).

☐ "Do not let immorality or any impurity or greed even be named among you" (5:3).

☐ "There must be no filthiness and silly talk, or coarse jesting, which are not fitting, but rather giving of thanks" (5:4).

☐ "Walk as children of light (for the fruit of the light consists in all goodness and righteousness and truth)" (5:8,9).

☐ "Do not participate in the unfruitful deeds of darkness, but instead even expose them" (5:11).

☐ "Be careful how you walk, not as unwise men, but as wise, making the most of your time" (5:15, 16).

☐ "Do not be foolish, but understand what the will of the Lord is" (5:17).

☐ "Do not get drunk with wine, for that is dissipation, but be filled with the Spirit" (5:18).

☐ "Be subject to one another in the fear of Christ" (5:21).

☐ "Wives, be subject to your own husbands, as to the Lord" (5:22).

☐ "Husbands, love your wives, just as Christ also loved the church" (5:25).

☐ "Children, obey your parents in the Lord" (6:1).

☐ "Fathers, do not provoke your children to anger; but bring them up in the discipline and instruction of the Lord" (6:4).

☐ "Slaves, be obedient to those who are your masters according to the flesh" (6:5).

☐ "Masters, do the same things to them" (6:9).

## A PERSONAL PROJECT

The following personal project is designed to help you develop the quality of "holiness" or Christ-likeness in your life.

### Step A

Using the previous verses from Paul's letter to the Ephesians, which describe practical holiness in a specific way, evaluate your own life. Use the list of exhortations as a criteria for spotting areas in your own life that need improvement. Place a check mark by those you need to give special attention.

### Step B

Translate each exhortation you check into personal goals in your own life. For example, if you have difficulty "loving your wife as Christ loved the church," your goals might look like this:

In order to love my wife as Christ loved the church, I have set up the following personal goals:

1. To be sensitive to her special emotional needs for security.

2. To set a proper example of Christ-likeness in handling all problems at home—especially in helping her with the children.

3. Spend more time with her, sharing my own life and communicating more effectively.

*Note:* Be specific in your goal-setting in relationship to your own set of circumstances and your own needs.

**Footnotes**

1. These words in 1 Thessalonians 2:10 are not only spoken of Paul's life but those of Timothy and Silas as well. Note the plural pronoun "we," and also compare with 1 Thessalonians 1:1.

21

NOT A NEW CONVERT

*An overseer must not be*
***a new convert****, lest he become*
*conceited and fall into the*
*condemnation incurred*
*by the devil.*
*1 Timothy 3:6*


One of the most tragic practices among Christian leaders in recent years is to encourage "new converts" to occupy "front-stage" positions in the evangelical world, and then to experience "instant popularity" as a Christian. This has been particularly true regarding individuals who have been prominent personalities: converted movie stars, musicians, athletes, etc. Perhaps another category is drug addicts, prostitutes, and any others who fall into the "chief of sinners" category.

Though the majority of Christian leaders who have done this no doubt mean well, unfortunately some seem to use this approach as a publicity tactic to attract large crowds for meetings or to demonstrate to "prospective donors" what God is doing through their organization.

Many new converts have survived this experience —thank God—but others have suffered shipwreck spiritually. The question is *why?*

Paul speaks of this issue clearly in 1 Timothy 3:7.

## PAUL'S PRIMARY CONCERN

Paul's basic concern in writing to Timothy, of course, is that Christian leaders should not appoint men to serve as elders who are "new converts." The word Paul uses here is *neophutos*. From it comes our English word "neophyte." Paul is saying that a man who is chosen to serve as a spiritual leader in the church should not be a "new Christian." The obvious implication is that no matter how zealous a man is or how sincere, no new Christian has sufficient experience to tackle the job of serving as an elder in the church. In other words, an elder must be a mature man of God.

Paul also tells *why* a Christian must be mature before he begins to serve as an elder in the church: "Not a new convert, lest he become conceited and fall into the condemnation incurred by the devil" (1 Tim. 3:6). To "become conceited" actually means to become blinded by pride, to lose perspective. More literally, Paul is saying that a new Christian can actually wrap himself in a "smoke screen of pride." And when this happens, says Paul, he will "fall into the condemnation incurred by the devil."

There is some question as to what Paul means by this statement. However, the most natural interpretation is that a man will receive the same kind of judgment Satan received because of *his* pride. Satan, you see, was originally a high-ranking angel serving in God's very presence. When he became proud and arrogant, he challenged God. He wanted to be like God. As a result, he fell from his lofty position (Isa. 14:12-14).

The following statement from Proverbs captures the intent of Paul's concern for a "new Christian" who may be appointed as an elder: "Pride goes before destruction, and a haughty spirit before stumbling" (16:18). Like Satan who fell, so a spiritual leader in the church can fall from his position because of pride.

It is important to emphasize that Paul's concern is that a new convert has not had time to develop the qualities of a mature man of God. He may have lots of experience in business, he may be highly skilled in some profession. Or he may be very talented as a musician, actor or sportsman. But he has not had opportunity nor time to develop a good reputation, to prove himself morally and ethically. As a Christian it takes time to develop prudence, respectability, an ability to teach, and uncontentiousness, to name a few of the qualities Paul lists which are marks of maturity. It takes time to learn the Scriptures and to develop "heavenly wisdom."

And if a man is converted who does not have his "household in order," it will probably take time to do so. In fact, the damage may be so great that the situation is irreparable. Consequently, in some cases, these men may have to be satisfied to develop all of the other traits of maturity, but realizing it would be unwise to serve as an elder in the church. This does not mean, however, he cannot become a mature man of God, demonstrating all of the other qualities. In fact, if there is any hope at all for "reconstructing a household," it is in developing these other qualities, which in turn will help a man communicate with those he has alienated.

## A BROADER APPLICATION

Though Paul is speaking of not appointing an *elder* who is a "new convert," there is a broader application. It is dangerous to give *any* new convert too much prominence as a Christian until he has developed certain marks of maturity. To do so is to contribute to his possible downfall; to help Satan get his foot in the door and create pride which eventually leads to personal downfall and failure.

This does not mean, of course, that a new Christian cannot participate as a member of the body of Christ, sharing his talents, his testimony and his life. But it does mean that over-exposure that focuses on the personality per se, can cause a person to become proud—to feel he is a "special gift" from God to the Christian community. Satan is just waiting, implies Paul, to take advantage of "new converts." And the apostle warns against "helping Satan along."

But there is an even broader application of Paul's concern in 1 Timothy 3:6. Though he is talking specifically about new converts, being a neophyte is not necessarily related to chronological age as a Christian. A man may have been a believer for many years and yet be immature and carnal. And in this state he is just as vulnerable to pride and its natural results as a new convert.

This, of course, is why Paul "spells out" how to recognize a mature man of God. For if he had simply said that a man could become an elder "after a certain period of time as a Christian," it would have opened the door to leaders who were yet babes in Christ.

Perhaps this is why there is no mention of elders in the Corinthian church. Perhaps after a year and a half of ministry among them, Paul still saw no one who was qualified. For in writing to them, he said: "And I, brethren, could not speak to you as to spiritual men, but as to men of flesh, as to babes in Christ. I gave you milk to drink, not solid food; for you were not yet able to receive it. Indeed, even now you are not yet able, for you are still fleshly" (1 Cor. 3:1-3).

And later in this letter Paul raises this question: "Is it so, that there is not among you one wise man . . . ?" (1 Cor. 6:5).

Paul makes it clear that while he was ministering among these Corinthians, he could not even teach them the deeper truths of God. They were too immature to understand it. And as he writes back to them, he still is unable to feed them "solid food" for they are still immature.

Consequently the first Corinthian letter in its totality deals primarily with problems reflecting childish and immature behavior among them—divisions (1), jealousy (3), pride (4), immorality (5), lawsuits (6), misuse of sex in marriage (7), idolatry (8-10), hair lengths (11), abuse of the Lord's supper (11), misuse of spiritual gifts—especially tongues (12-

14), and doubts about the Resurrection, without which true Christianity cannot exist (15).

These truly are marks of *immaturity*—both in the body of Christ and among individuals—rather than marks of maturity.

## THE PROBLEM OF PRIDE

At the heart of Paul's concern in 1 Timothy 3:6 is pride, "lest he become conceited." Paul uses the same basic word in 1 Timothy 6:3,4: "If anyone advocates a different doctrine, and does not agree with sound words, those of our Lord Jesus Christ, and with the doctrine conforming to godliness, he is conceited and understands nothing. . . ."

Pride has ruined many people. It was a major sin in Israel's history, for when they entered the land and "received for nothing" all of the natural blessings God gave them, they took credit for it themselves (Deut. 8:14; Judg. 2:10). Later Uzziah was severely judged by God because "when he became strong, his heart was so proud that he acted corruptly . . ." (2 Chron. 26:16). And Hezekiah, too, was judged "because his heart was proud" (2 Chron. 32:25). But when he "humbled the pride of his heart" he was again blessed by God (2 Chron. 32:26-33).

Both James and Peter writing in the New Testament make reference to Proverbs 3:24 when they said: "God is opposed to the proud, but gives grace to the humble" (Jas. 4:6; 1 Pet. 5:5).

Any Christian, no matter how mature, can become a victim of Satan's darts in this area of his life. And how much more so a new Christian? How easy it is to become proud of human accomplishments—to take credit for what belongs to God. Since the dawn of Christianity man has even consistently tried to take credit for his salvation, which leads to pride and self-righteousness. Thus Paul wrote, "For by grace you have been saved through faith; and that not of yourselves, it is the gift of God; not as a result of works, that no one should boast" (Eph. 2:8-9).

## THE SOURCE OF PRIDE

Satan, obviously, is the ultimate source of pride. We have often heard that we secretly—or not so secretly—enjoy seeing others fail in the areas of our own greatest weakness. Thus Satan gets great satisfaction in seeing Christians fail in the area that caused him to lose his position in God's presence.

But there is also another explanation for a tendency toward pride. In some people, it has more human causes. These causes relate to the same factors as those creating a problem for some in the area of anger, self-will, an argumentative spirit, an inordinate desire for money, and even addicton to alcohol, or other things. The root cause is a psychological one relating to how much attention a person has received as a child. Too much attention, of course, can create a "spoiled child." But strange as it may seem, "not enough attention" can also create a problem—a problem with pride.

For example, a person who does not receive enough attention develops a tremendous thirst for attention. Later in life, when he eventually gets attention that comes naturally from achievement, he has never learned how to handle this success emotionally. Consequently he may go through life constantly fighting a pride problem, inwardly desiring to take an undue amount of credit for what he thinks are his accomplishments. The strange thing is that people with this tendency often become proud over practically nothing. They tend to over-interpret and exaggerate their accomplishments.

How important it is, then, for fathers and mothers to create a balanced environment where the needs of a child, physically and psychologically, are met in order that he may eventually become a spiritually mature individual.

## A PERSONAL PROJECT

The following project is designed to help you evaluate your maturity level as a Christian. Are you still a "babe in Christ" even though you may have been a Christian for several years?

### Step A

This is basically a review project. The following questions and evaluation scale will help you to rate yourself in relationship to the qualities we have studied. Circle the number that best represents your self-evaluation, rating from dissatisfied (1) to satisfied (7).

1. How do you evaluate your reputation as a Christian?

Dissatisfied   1   2   3   4   5   6   7   Satisfied

**2.** How do you evaluate your overall relationship with your wife? And if you are not married, how well are you handling your sexual problems?

Dissatisfied   1   2   3   4   5   6   7   Satisfied

**3.** What kind of overall perspective do you have on the Christian life? In other words, have you developed a biblical philosophy of life? Does it reflect *temperance?*

Dissatisfied   1   2   3   4   5   6   7   Satisfied

**4.** Are you *prudent?* That is, do you have a correct view of yourself in relationship to other Christians? In relationship to God?

Dissatisfied   1   2   3   4   5   6   7   Satisfied

**5.** Are you *respectable?* Do you have a well-adjusted life, adorning the Word of God?

Dissatisfied   1   2   3   4   5   6   7   Satisfied

**6.** Are you *hospitable?* Do you use your home as a means to minister to other members of the body of Christ as well as to non-Christians?

Dissatisfied   1   2   3   4   5   6   7   Satisfied

**7.** Are you *able to teach?* That is, do you have that quality of life that enables you to communicate the Word of God to others in a non-argumentative manner?

Dissatisfied   1   2   3   4   5   6   7   Satisfied

**8.** Are you *addicted to anything that is controlling your life?* Furthermore, are you doing anything that is causing a weaker Christian to stumble and sin against God?

Dissatisfied  1  2  3  4  5  6  7  Satisfied

9. Are you *self-willed?* That is, do you always have to have your own way?

Dissatisfied  1  2  3  4  5  6  7  Satisfied

10. Do you *lose your temper* easily? Do you harbor feelings of resentment over a period of time? Or are you in control of this area of your life?

Dissatisfied  1  2  3  4  5  6  7  Satisfied

11. Are you a *pugnacious* type person—one who physically strikes out at others because of angry feelings? Or are you in control of this area of your life?

Dissatisfied  1  2  3  4  5  6  7  Satisfied

12. Are you *contentious?* That is, do you purposely take the opposite point of view from others, stirring up arguments and destroying the unity in the group? Or are you a "peacemaker" striving to create harmony and unity?

Dissatisfied  1  2  3  4  5  6  7  Satisfied

13. Are you a *mild-mannered* and *gentle* person, reflecting meekness, forbearance, and kindness?

Dissatisfied  1  2  3  4  5  6  7  Satisfied

14. Are you *free from the love of money?* That is, do you seek first His kingdom and His righteousness?

Dissatisfied  1  2  3  4  5  6  7  Satisfied

15. Do you have your *household in order?* That is, do your wife and children love and respect you and are they responding to your God and Saviour and His claim on their lives?

Dissatisfied  1  2  3  4  5  6  7  Satisfied

16. Do you have a *good reputation* with non-Christians? That is, do they respect you even though they may disagree with your religious views?

Dissatisfied  1  2  3  4  5  6  7  Satisfied

17. Do you *pursue after that which is good and right?* Do you desire to associate yourself with truth, honor, and integrity?

Dissatisfied  1  2  3  4  5  6  7  Satisfied

18. Are you *just?* That is, are you able to make objective decisions and be honest in your relationship with other people?

Dissatisfied  1  2  3  4  5  6  7  Satisfied

19. Are you *pursuing after personal and practical holiness?*

Dissatisfied  1  2  3  4  5  6  7  Satisfied

20. Are you in the process of *continual growth in your Christian life,* becoming more and more like Jesus Christ?

Dissatisfied  1  2  3  4  5  6  7  Satisfied

## Step B
Now go back and check those items that you cir-

cled that have the lowest numbers. Set up a priority list for *personal action.*